Talking About Statis

Testing and Statistics

Talking About Statistics

A Psychologist's Guide to Data Analysis

Brian S Everitt
Professor of Statistics in Behavioural Science, Institute of Psychiatry, London.

and

Dale F Hay
Senior Lecturer, Institute of Psychiatry, London.

Edward Arnold
A division of Hodder & Stoughton
LONDON MELBOURNE AUCKLAND

Copublished in the Americas by Halsted Press
an imprint of John Wiley & Sons Inc.
New York — Toronto

© 1992 B.S. Everitt and D.F. Hay

First published in Great Britain 1992

Copublished in the Americas by Halsted Press, an imprint of John Wiley & Sons Inc., 605 Third Avenue, New York, NY 10158

British Library Cataloguing in Publication Data

Everitt, Brian
   Talking About Statistics: Psychologist's Guide to
   Design and Analysis
   I. Title II. Hay, Dale F.
   519.5

   ISBN 0340 52921 0

Library of Congress Cataloging-in-Publication Data

Available upon request.

   ISBN 0 470 21956 4

Printed and bound in Great Britain for Edward Arnold, a division of Hodder and Stoughton Limited, Mill Road, Dunton Green, Sevenoaks, Kent TN13 2YA, by the University Press, Cambridge.

Preface

This book is intended for psychologists who have had an introduction to statistics and research design at the undergraduate level. It should be well suited for the postgraduate student who is learning about advanced statistical techniques before undertaking Ph.D.-level research. Because the book is organised in terms of a series of research questions that lead systematically one from another, and because the entire book is based on an extended example, it should be a useful supplement to a more traditional statistical text.

In addition, our book should also be helpful to psychological researchers who have been working in the field for some time, and who learned their statistical methods a while ago. Such workers may feel, as the second author does, that their postgraduate training no longer equips them to cope with newer statistical techniques such as logistic regression, structural equation models, and the like. This book thus provides a refresher course for the working psychologist.

In the chapters that follow, we illustrate some of the most common types of research designs a psychologist would employ, by describing an extended programme of research on a clinical issue, namely, the impact of a mother's depression on her child's development and well-being. The organisation of the book emphasises the way in which a researcher's decisions to ask particular questions and use particular measures almost completely determine the nature of the statistical analysis to be undertaken. We introduce each statistical technique as it would logically arise over time, in a systematic programme of research, with recurring consultation sessions between the psychologist and the statistician. We have stressed the advantages of consultation with a statistician in the early phases of a project, as well as during the last, frantic stage of data analysis.

Because we wish to emphasise ways in which problems of communication between a psychologist and a statistician can be resolved, the text is written in dialogue format. We refer to the psychologist and statistician as "Frances" and "Sidney" respectively, and see them as caricatures of ourselves. (We would like to think that Frances is a bit more naive and Sidney a bit more pompous in his speech than are their real-life prototypes!) In the course of their dialogue, the psychologist poses a specific question, which the statistician then attempts to answer.

The psychologist on occasion then attempts to clarify the statistician's remarks, either by re-phrasing them in non-mathematical terms or by providing a concrete example. We are all too aware that the dialogue format may become a bit tedious; however, we believe that it serves a useful pedagogical function, breaking down the material into a series of particular topics that are framed by Frances's questions. This allows us to introduce quite technical material in a series of manageable steps. Thus we hope the reader will bear with the slightly embarrassing qualities of the dialogue.

The choice of a dialogue format is also directed at another objective: We hope that the reader will go through the book as if it were a novel, reading the chapters in chronological order, and noting how, as in any programme of resarch, initial decisions influence subsequent possibilities for analysis. We begin the story, as with any reasonable novel (we are not post-modernists!) at the beginning, with the psychologist approaching the statistician before undertaking an extensive programme of research. We have deliberately chosen an example that illustrates many of the pitfalls faced when doing clinically relevant research. Thus Frances and Sidney must negotiate their ways around problems of inadequate sample sizes, time-consuming experimental manipulations and measurement, missing data, and the like.

All the examples in the chapters that follow are based on two data sets. One represents a prior study, the results of which Frances examines before planning her own prevention study. Because real data best illustrate the problems any statistician and psychologist encounter, the first data set comes from an actual study of the long-term effects of a mother's postnatal depression on her child's development. We are deeply grateful to Dr. R. Kumar for allowing us to present selected findings from his longitudinal study of postnatal depression (e.g., Coghill, Caplan, Alexandra, Robson and Kumar, 1986) to illustrate various statistical points.

The second data set, which represents Frances's own attempt to use experimental methods to prevent the occurrence of postnatal depression and to alleviate its effects on children, is entirely fictional. It presents different sorts of variables, measured on different scales, posing particular problems for the data analyst. It is our hope that, by using a common theme throughout the book, and by restricting our examples to two data sets, the reader will be able to follow a logical sequence of questions that inexorably leads to a logical choice of statistical techniques.

Throughout the book, we have presented the logic of what Frances and Sidney are doing in their conversations. A more mathematical exposition of the various analytic techniques is presented in a series of displays that are interspersed throughout the text. The reader is thus advised to read through the dialogue in each section of each chapter, and then consult the associated displays for a detailed account of the statistical procedures under discussion.

Contents

1

Why Can't a Psychologist Be More Like a Statistician? (And vice versa)

1.1   Introduction

Have you heard the one about the psychologist who carried out 100 t-tests and 50 chi-squared tests when comparing two treatment groups, each containing 10 patients? And have you heard about the psychologist who asked for help in interpreting 200 pages of output from a factor analysis on a 150-item questionnaire given to 20 subjects? On the other hand, have you heard about the statistician whose recommendations that data be analysed in the newest, most up-to-date ways possible routinely led to problems in getting the eventual manuscript accepted for publication?

Over the course of the last 50 years, the psychologist has become a voracious consumer of statistical methods, but the relationship between psychologist and statistician is not always an easy, happy or fruitful one. Statisticians complain that psychologists put undue faith in significance tests, often use complex methods of analysis when the data merit only a relatively simple approach and in general abuse many statistical techniques. Additionally, many statisticians feel that psychologists have become too easily seduced by user-friendly statistical software. These statisticians are upset (and perhaps even a little threatened) when their advice to "plot a few graphs" is ignored in favour of a multivariate analysis of covariance or similar statistical extravagance.

But if statisticians are at times horrified by the way in which psychologists apply statistical techniques, psychologists are no less horrified by many statisticians' apparent lack of awareness of what psychological research requires. A statistician may demand a balanced design with 30 subjects in each cell, so as to achieve some appropriate power for the analysis. But it is not the statistician who is faced with the frustration caused by a last-minute phone call from a subject who cannot take part in an experiment that has taken several hours to arrange. The statistician advising on a longitudinal study may call for more effort in carrying out follow-up interviews, so that no subjects are missed. It is, however, the psychologist who must continue to persuade people to talk about potentially distressing aspects of their lives, who must confront possibly dangerous respondents, or who arrives at a given address to conduct an interview, only to find that the person is not at home. In general, statisticians do not appear to appreciate the complex stories lying behind each data point in a psychological study.

How, then, can the statistician and psychologist even begin to converse, let alone enter into a mutually agreeable collaboration? There are clear advantages for both in talking to each other. Most psychologists pursuing their own ideas meet statistical problems that require some sort of emergency treatment. Many of these could easily have been averted by consulting with the statistician beforehand. On the other hand, left to their own devices, it is not unknown for statisticians to perform analyses that are statistically sound but psychologically naive or even misleading. For example, one of the authors once heard an accomplished statistician propose an interpretation of findings regarding the benefits of nursery education, in which all subsequent positive effects could be accounted for in terms of the parents' choice of primary school. For once, it was the psychologists who turned to exchange knowing looks: In the country under discussion, parents typically do not have any opportunity to choose the schools their children attend!

Before we can suggest ways of overcoming the communication problems between psychologist and statistician, we must identify some sources of the problems. Initially it is helpful to consider the interaction between psychologist and statistician in historical perspective, and so we begin our book with a little history.

1.2   A Little History

The relationship between psychology and statistics is a necessary one. A widely quoted remark by Galton states "that until the phenomena of any branch of knowledge have been submitted to measurement and number, it cannot assume the dignity of a science." And Galton was not alone in demanding measurement and numbers as a *sine qua non* for attaining the dignity of a science. Lord Kelvin is quoted as saying that one cannot understand a phenomenon until it is subjected to measurement, and Thorndike has said that whatever exists, exists in some amount, and therefore could eventually be subjected to measurement and counting.

Psychology has long striven to attain "the dignity of a science" by submitting its observations to measurement and quantification. According to Singer (1979), David Hartley (1705–1757), in his major work, *Observations on Man* (1749), discussed the relevance of probability theory to the collection of scientific evidence, and argued for the use of mathematical and statistical ideas in the study of psychological processes. Later Fechner (1801–1887) and Quetelet (1796–1874) introduced the ideas of measures of association, but it was perhaps Galton (1822–1911), of all these early workers, who was most responsible for demonstrating the usefulness of statistical methods in psychology and for developing statistical techniques applicable to psychological problems. Of particular note was Galton's introduction of a mathematical aid, borrowed from J. D. H. Dickson, in his study of "regression toward mediocrity." This was the *index of correlation*, later christened by Edgeworth in 1892, the *coefficient of correlation*. A suitable statistical theory for this coefficient was later developed by Pearson.

One of the reasons why we are adopting an historical perspective at this point in the text is to try to highlight sources of the apparent communications gap between many psychologists and statisticians. As we see it, psychologists are largely unaware of the history of statistical theory and its current status as a lively science that is continuing to undergo rapid development: They tend to see a finite set of statistical techniques graven in stone. On the other hand, statisticians are not aware that the extreme allegiance certain psychologists show to a few favoured statistical techniques has its roots in a basic schism between experimental psychologists and psychometricians that occurred in the 1920s and 1930s. This historical divide still has implications for psychologists' ability to grasp new developments in statistical theory. These differences become clearer when we focus on a particular set of issues: the use of experimental vs. non-experimental designs for addressing psychological questions about cause and effect.

1.2.1 The "Two Sciences of Psychology": Experimentation vs. Correlation

As long ago as 1957, Cronbach drew attention to the existence of two quite separate "disciplines of scientific psychology." One sort of psychologist attempts to test general principles about human and animal behaviour, and is concerned with documenting average performance; the other sort of psychologist is interested in describing and interpreting individual differences, in particular with respect to various dimensions of intellectual ability, personality, and psychopathology. The first sort of psychologist does experiments, typically on small samples obtained for reasons of convenience. The other sort of psychologist does larger-scale questionnaire surveys or interview studies, attempts to procure representative samples, and tends to use standardised, pre-validated measures. When analysing results, the first sort of psychologist tends to compute t-tests and analyses of variance. The second sort tends to use correlation, regression, and factor-analytic techniques. Thus two historically separate areas of substantive inquiry within psychology have been linked to different aspects of statistical theory.

A long-standing tradition in scientific psychology is the application of John Stuart Mill's experimental "method of difference" to the study of psychological problems. Groups of subjects are compared who theoretically differ with respect to the experimental treatment, but otherwise are the same in all other respects. Any difference in outcome can therefore be attributed to the treatment. Control procedures such as randomisation or matching on potentially confounding variables help bolster the assumption that the groups are the same in everything except the treatment conditions.

This experimental tradition has long been wedded to a particular statistical technique, namely, the analysis of variance. The principles of experimental design and the analysis of variance were developed primarily by Fisher in the 1920s, but took some time to be fully appreciated by psychologists. Psychologists continued to analyse their experimental data with a mixture of graphical and simple statistical methods until well into the 1930s. According to Lovie (1979), the earliest paper that had "ANOVA" in its title was by Gaskill and Cox (1937). Other early uses of the technique are reported in Crutchfield (1938, 1939) and Crutchfield and Tolman (1940).

Several of these early psychological papers, although paying lip service to the use of Fisher's analysis of variance techniques, relied heavily on more informal strategies of inference in interpreting experimental results. The year 1940, however, saw a dramatic increase in the use of analysis of variance in the psychological literature, and, by 1943, the review paper of Garrett and Zubin was able to cite over 40 studies using analysis of variance or covariance in psychology and education. Since then, of course, the analysis of variance in all its guises has become the main technique used in experimental psychology. For example, examination of two years of issues of the *British Journal of Psychology* showed that over 50% of the papers contain one or other application of the analysis of variance, the majority of such analyses being reported in the standard tabular format recommended by Winer (1971).

What statisticians find strange about psychologists' fascination with the analysis of variance is not so much inappropriate application of a statistical technique (though such applications do occur). What seems strange is the impression given by psychologists that there have been no developments in statistical science since 1940, that the analysis of variance procedure was delivered on tablets of stone in the 1920s to remain unchanged for the rest of time.

In fact, this particular area of statistical theory has seen many changes and developments over the last two decades. Improved methods for the analysis of repeated measures designs have, for example, been developed. Furthermore, procedures to apply analysis of variance-type forms of inference to data that do not meet its usual assumptions are now routine. The development of the *generalised linear model* approach (see Nelder and McCullagh, 1990) has seen the introduction of methods of analysis suitable for response variables that fall into discrete categories, data that previously would have been analysed by techniques such as chi square. Clearly, simple analysis of variance designs, as described by Winer (1971), are no longer "state of the art."

It is not, of course, true that all psychologists are ignorant of these statistical developments. However, the attraction to novelty shown by some psychologists raises additional problems for the statistician. Often, in their haste to be at the forefront in the application of new methodology, psychologists have applied the new techniques themselves in a less than sensible manner. This problem is exacerbated by the availability of new, powerful statistical packages, containing exotic types of analyses that can be performed on the desktop computer. The availability of such user-friendly packages has probably decreased the likelihood of psychologists seeking advice from statisticians at exactly the time when the psychologists are trying their hands at more complicated statistical techniques. For many statisticians, this has confirmed a further prejudice, namely, that the psychologist often is an unthinking "follower of fashion" as far as statistical analyses are concerned.

How, then, can psychologists best acquaint themselves with new statistical developments and go beyond the safe confines of familiar analysis of variance techniques? How can statisticians best help them develop their skills in this way? This is where adoption of an historical perspective may help the statistician as well as the psychologist. Consider, for example, the fact that psychologists may seem slow to grasp the generalised linear model approach. Statisticians find this bewildering; can't these mathematically and statistically feckless individuals grasp the fact that their hallowed analysis of variance technique is simply regression with dummy variables, and thus just one example of the more general linear model?

Here it is the statistician who has not taken an historical perspective, and fails to grasp the fact that the two different sorts of psychologists are often quite ignorant of each other's approaches. The experimental psychologist may not only glorify ANOVA, but may in fact never have had any reason or opportunity to learn about other sorts of statistical designs. It is the second sort of psychologist, the psychometrician interested in individual differences, who is more aware of correlational techniques and is better able to grasp the newer approaches. These divergent intellectual traditions within psychology constrain research decisions and lead to some resistance to new ideas. The statistician is well advised to start the consultation process from a point that reflects the background and expertise of the psychologist, and draws upon a logic with which that particular psychologist is already familiar.

1.2.2   "Latent" Variables and Finding Causes without Experimentation

The need for integration of the experimental and correlational traditions is nowhere more evident than in the recent efforts to draw reliable causal inferences from correlational data. In the past, psychologists have taken it as an article of faith that only experimental studies can demonstrate cause and effect relationships. Now, however, developments in statistical theory have raised new possibilities for the study of psychological issues that are difficult to tackle with the experimental method. Historically, these developments derive from the "other sort of psychology" of the psychometricians, and thus the experimental psychologist is often singularly unprepared to appreciate these new possibilities.

We noted earlier that the concept of a coefficient of correlation expressing a relationship between two variables was introduced by Galton in the 19th century. The introduction of this concept was closely followed by the basic ideas of what we now generally refer to as *factor analysis*. For example, Spearman suggested that the correlation between two variables signified the existence of an underlying common factor. This logic was extended by the psychometric theorists of the 1920s and 1930s, who were interested in investigating individual differences on such general, unseen traits as intelligence or various aspects of personality. Whereas the behaviourists and the experimental psychologists tended to see the human mind as a "black box," and restricted their attention to observable behaviours (such as pressing a button in a learning task), the "other sort of psychologists" saw the correlation coefficient as a key into the mysteries of personality and mental life. They equated the "common factors" derived from a matrix of correlations with psychological traits that could be given meaningful names, for example intelligence or personality.

The idea of using correlations between *observed* variables, such as scores on a standardised intelligence test like the ones being developed by Binet in the early 20th century, to identify an unobservable or *latent* variable as emotive as intelligence soon became an area of increasing controversy. Initially, the major arguments occurred between psychologists such as Spearman, Thomson and Thurstone. But statisticians could not resist becoming involved. Most statisticians were clearly sceptical, particularly because of the non-identifiability (in mathematical terms) of the analyses used to identify common factors, and because the process of rotating the factors until they looked meaningful seemed to allow researchers to impose their own prejudices on the data.

Other statisticians, however, took a more constructive view of the emerging work on factor analysis, and perceived that the psychologists' use of the technique presented a challenge to statistical theory which they should take up. However, it was not until the development of powerful computers that statistically more respectable methods of performing a factor analysis became feasible. Before this relatively recent development, the computational problems for early workers applying the methods of factor analysis must have been considerable. Maxwell (personal communication) tells the story of Godfrey Thomson's approach to the arithmetical problems faced when performing a factor analysis by hand. According to Maxwell, Godfrey Thomson and his wife would, early in the evening, place themselves on either side of their sitting room fire, Mr. Thomson equipped with several pencils and much paper, and Mrs. Thomson with a copy of Barlow's multiplication tables. For several hours, the conversation would consist of little more than "What's 613.23 multiplied by 714.62?" "438134.44"; "What's 904.72 divided by 986.31?" "0.91728", etc., etc.! Those of us who still remember using mechanical computing machines, slide rules and tables of square roots, and who recall the chaos engendered by spilling decks of computer cards on the floor, are perhaps best able to appreciate the technological revolution that has transformed both statistical theory and empirical psychology in the last two decades.

With the technological advances in computing has come an extension of the factor analysis logic into more powerful statistical theory, particularly as developed by Jöreskog, Browne and Bentler. These developments have led to the use of "structural equation models" which permit quite complicated hypothesis testing in the context of non-experimental data. The importance of these recent developments in statistical theory cannot be underestimated by the psychologist: According to one scholar, "The development of the rigorous and generalized methods for testing hypotheses concerning underlying structures in covariance matrices is perhaps the most important and influential statistical revolution to have occurred in the social sciences" (Cliff, 1983).

The suggestion that one need not conduct experiments to make causal inferences, combined with the arrival of well-documented and forcefully marketed computer software that makes it all possible and relatively simple, has been hard for psychologists to resist. Unfortunately, many psychologists appear to have suspended their usual critical faculties in the initial wave of enthusiasm for structural equation models. The old, but still apposite aphorism, "Correlation does not imply causation," once chanted by generations of experimental psychologists, appears to have been somewhat forgotten amongst the mass of path diagrams, parameter estimates and models for everything from theories of intelligence to sexual behaviour. Reification is rife: Latent variables are given names and tested as if they had an independent existence and might even be directly manipulable, if necessary. In many cases, little attention is given to the purpose that the causal model finally adopted is intended to serve.

All of this is, of course, an extremely unsatisfactory state of affairs, and statisticians are not loath to say so. Recent uses and abuses of structural equation models seem, to many statisticians, just more in a long line of psychologists' misusing complicated statistical techniques.

Furthermore, once again they fear that psychologists have been too easily seduced by the commercial statistical packages. As Cliff (1983) remarked,

> "Beautiful computer programs do not really change anything fundamental. Correlation data are still correlational and no computer program can take account of variables that are not in the analysis. Causal relations can only be established through patient, painstaking attention to all the relevant variables, and should involve active manipulation as a final confirmation."

In other words, the skills of the experimental psychologist in designing simple tests of clear hypotheses are not yet out of date. In general, the two types of psychologists Cronbach (1957) identified have tended to show equally important but non-overlapping strengths. The correlational psychologist whose work is steeped in the psychometric tradition has been best prepared to appreciate the new advances in statistical theory, largely because such psychologists have already been dealing with the concept of latent variables for decades. Since the early part of this century, psychometricians have been concerned to document the reliability and validity of their measurements of general constructs such as intelligence or personality, as inferred from standardised assessment tools. In classical test theory they distinguished between true scores, in terms of the theoretical construct, and observed scores, in terms of the actual testing instrument, contaminated as it was with measurement error. They have also been particularly keen to obtain representative samples, again to reduce measurement error, and have thus found epidemiological sampling methods relatively easy to take on board.

In contrast, the experimental tradition has been quite cavalier in its choice of measures and in its attention to sampling issues. In a recent survey of one volume of the *Journal of Experimental Psychology*, it was found that no article even mentioned the validity of the measures. Indeed, in such studies, dependent variables seem to be taken at face value, and no attempt is made to estimate the error of their measurement of latent constructs. Issues of the representativeness of the samples used also tend to be down-played. The strengths of the experimental approach, however, lie in the close attention paid to the logic of causal inference and, in particular, the setting up of alternative hypotheses that need to be addressed through particular control procedures. Such a logical approach is required in non-experimental attempts to make causal inferences as well, and, in the light of recent statistical developments, it is more necessary than ever for the two traditions within psychology to become integrated. We have thus aimed to present the topics discussed within this book in a way that promotes such integration.

1.2.3 Drawing Conclusions from Data: Going Beyond the Significance Test

One particular way in which the logic of experimental design has pervaded all of psychology, even work that falls within the correlational and factor analytic tradition, is in regard to psychologists' obsession with the significance test. It is hard for most statisticians to understand the sanctity with which significance tests are regarded in the psychological literature. Again, a historical perspective is perhaps useful here.

The first published use of reasoning that resembles a significance test is commonly attributed to John Arbuthnot (1710), and involved a comparison of male and female births in London in each of 82 years when birth records were kept. He calculated, on the assumption of equal chance of a male or female being born at any given birth, that the observed finding in all 82 years of an excess of male births was exceedingly improbable. Another early example of something akin to a significance test was Mitchell's (1767) argument that the stars were not distributed at random. It was much later, however, that Edgeworth (1885) introduced a procedure that most present day psychologists would see as a relatively accurate description of their approach to inference:

"In order to determine whether the difference between two proposed means is or is not accidental, form the probability curve under which the said difference, supposing it were accidental, would range. Consider whether the difference between the observed means exceeds two to three times the modules of that curve. If it does, the difference is not accidental."

Later, Edgeworth described such a result as *significant*.

It was in the 1890s that statisticians began to develop the tests in use today, such as the chi-squared and *t*-tests. In the 1920s workers such as Fisher, Neyman and Pearson created various testing methodologies. Since then, the significance test, in all its manifestations, has been well and truly adopted by the psychologist. The psychological literature is littered with the results of various sorts of tests, and, in addition, is often liberally decorated with asterisks (*, **, or even ***) to denote varying degrees of statistical significance. (Sprent, in 1970, commented that the "star" nomenclature is more suited to a hotel guide book than a serious scientific paper). Thirty years ago Sterling (1959) found that approximately 80% of the articles in psychological journals used significance tests. More recently, Oakes (1979) has shown that such tests are now, if anything, more prevalent in the psychological literature. We should note that the reliance on significance testing is not restricted to the experimental literature, where the setting of specific decision criteria *a priori* is part of the overall logic of the research design. Significance tests are used as well in quasi-experimental designs, for example, where a clinical group is being compared with matched control subjects, and often significance tests are all psychologists note from the results of regression analyses.

Apparently the significance test satisfies the need of a researcher who is searching for a way to distinguish between "weighty" and "less weighty" findings. But is such enthusiasm for the ubiquitous significance test entirely justified? Many statisticians, and not a few psychologists, would say "No." For example, Skipper *et al.* (1967) comment:

> "The current obsession with 0.05, it would seem, has the consequence of differentiating significant research findings from those best forgotten, published studies from unpublished ones, and renewal of grants from termination. It would not be difficult to document the joy experienced by a social scientist when his *F* ratio or *t*-value yields significance at 0.05, nor his horror when the table reads only 0.10 or 0.06. One comes to internalise the difference between 0.05 and 0.06 as 'right' or 'wrong,' 'creditable' vs. 'embarrassing,' 'success' vs. 'failure.'"

Many statisticians (e.g., Gardner and Altman, 1989; Oakes, 1986) argue strongly for the replacement of significance tests by estimation and confidence intervals. But such arguments appear to have had little impact in psychology where the editorial policies of many psychological journals still demand *p*-values. Such demands might be less irritating for statisticians, despite their preference for other methods of drawing conclusions from data, if there was evidence that psychologists knew exactly what they were doing when conducting significance tests. But, sadly, Oakes (1986) presented a simple test to 70 academic psychologists, and found that only 3 could properly interpret the result of a simple *t*-test. This was not particularly encouraging, given that the subjects in the study were all university lecturers, research fellows or postgraduate students with at least two years' research experience! (You can see how well you do on Oakes' test when you get to Chapter 3).

To address this particularly difficult communication problem between psychologist and statistician, we shall review the logic of significance testing associated with various research designs, but we shall also emphasise alternative ways of drawing conclusions from data.

1.3   Plan of the Book

In Chapter 2, before designing her own study, Frances presents Sidney with some relevant data from a previous study. Methods of displaying and summarising these data are discussed.

In Chapter 3, the problems of designing Frances' proposed prevention study are addressed. Hypotheses are formulated and calculations performed to assess the number of subjects she will need.

Chapter 4 deals with the selection of outcome variables and issues of measurement and reliability.

In Chapter 5, Frances and Sidney consider ways in which two groups can be compared. Simple significance tests are discussed and Sidney introduces Frances to the advantages of a confidence interval approach.

Nonparametric and multivariate procedures for comparing two groups are also discussed.

Chapter 6 looks at the ways in which more than two groups can be compared along one or more dimensions. Analysis of variance procedures, both univariate and multivariate, are presented and their relation to multiple regression procedures discussed.

In Chapter 7, Frances shows Sidney data from her longitudinal study and repeated measure designs are discussed.

Chapter 8 introduces the problems of analysing data involving a categorical response variable.

In Chapter 9, factor analysis and more general latent variable models are discussed with respect to assessing what experimental and non-experimental variables determine child outcome in the study.

With this plan in mind, we now turn to a scene in a dimly lit corridor of a university statistics department. Where years ago there would have been the cheerful clattering of mechanical calculators, there is now only a ghostly hush. The psychologist knocks tentatively on the statistican's door ...

2

Examining Some Pilot Data: A Review of Basic Descriptive Statistics

2.1 Introduction

Most research projects do not arise *de novo*; rather, new hypotheses are generated on the basis of past work, and there is a cumulative progression of knowledge over time. In some cases researchers are fortunate enough to be able actually to examine data collected in previous studies with some care, before formulating their own hypotheses. This acquaints the researcher with characteristics of the population to be studied and, in particular, with the nature of the data that are likely to be collected in future studies. In this chapter, we have imagined the situation where a researcher has been given the opportunity to examine the findings from an existing study on the same topic, namely, the effects of a mother's postnatal depression on her child's development.

Once a set of data has been collected, coded and put into a file on a computer, investigators are often eager to plunge directly into testing particular hypotheses or assessing specific models, without paying too much attention to the simpler (but nonetheless important) aspects of their data. Such an approach is not to be recommended. Instead, investigators should examine their data very carefully in an attempt to uncover patterns, and check that the distributions of scores they are about to analyse meet the assumptions of the analysis they plan to conduct. In this chapter, Sidney is urging Frances to take such a careful look at the existing data, before attempting to design her own study. Their conversations provide a review of basic descriptive statistics, with which the reader is probably already familiar, but also a description of some more recently developed methods for examining data.

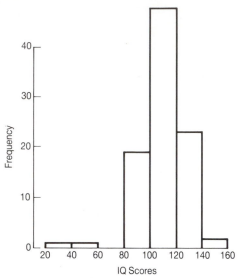

Display 2.1   Histogram of Child IQ Scores

FRANCES

You will recall that I thought I'd start this project with a look at the sorts of effects postnatal depression might be expected to have on children's development. Because I'm just beginning to design my own prevention study, and it will be some years before the outcome is fully known, I think it would be useful to take a careful look at some findings that have already been obtained. One of my colleagues and his associates (Coghill et al., 1986) conducted a prospective study of mothers who gave birth to their firstborn children in a major teaching hospital in London. Amongst other things, they measured the mother's mental state 3 months after childbirth, and tested the child's IQ some 4 years later. In addition, at the age 4 interview they asked mothers about the children's behavioural problems. I'd like to look at the IQ scores of the children of depressed and non-depressed mothers.

SIDNEY

Before looking at differences between the children of depressed and well women, we really should make a preliminary examination of the IQ scores for the sample as a whole. Is the IQ score on the usual scale? Is the mean expected to be 100?

FRANCES

Yes. Here are the data and a histogram I've constructed. (For the data see Appendix A—For the histogram see Display 2.1).

SIDNEY

Although the histogram is quite a useful way of displaying a distribution of scores, I prefer to begin by constructing a suitable stem-and-leaf plot. Have you done this yet?

FRANCES
I'm not even sure that I know what you mean.

2.2 Checking the "Shape" of Individual Variables: Stem-and-Leaf Displays

SIDNEY
In the past, people have examined the distributional properties of variables informally, by making plots and diagrams such as histograms, bar charts, frequency polygons and the like. These kinds of diagrams are still useful, but they've now been largely superseded by what's known as a *stem-and-leaf plot*, introduced by Tukey in the 1970s (Tukey, 1970, 1972). Such a plot allows a set of variable values to be organised graphically in a way that directs attention to particular features of the data, such as

(a)   how nearly symmetric the distribution is,
(b)   how spread out the scores are,
(c)   whether a few values are far removed from the rest,
(d)   whether there are concentrations of data,
(e)   whether there are gaps in the data.

The stem-and-leaf display does not set forth any elaborate theory, but provides a flexible, effective technique for a preliminary look at samples of data. The data values themselves do most of the work of sorting the sample into numerical order and displaying it.

To construct the simplest form of stem-and-leaf display we begin by choosing a suitable pair of adjacent digits in the data—in our example the tens digit and the units digit. Next we split each data value between these two digits (see Display 2.2). Then we allocate a separate line in the display for each possible string of leading digits (the *stem*). Finally we write down the trailing digit (the *leaf*) of each data value on the line corresponding to its leading digit.

The stem-and-leaf display for the IQ data (see Display 2.2) resembles a histogram with an interval width of 10 IQ points; the leaves add numerical detail and the plot preserves all the information in the data.

The stem-and-leaf display shows that the bulk of the children have IQ scores between 90 and 120, although there are a considerable proportion in this sample that have scores higher than 120. Only a few children have scores below 90, and one child has an extremely low IQ value, a point that needs to be kept in mind as we examine these data again later.

FRANCES
Given that eventually I'm going to be interested in comparing two groups of children within this sample, those whose mothers are depressed postnatally and those whose mothers are well in the first year, should we construct two separate stem-and-leaf plots? And, if so, how should I compare them, given

---

Display 2.2 Stem-and-Leaf Plots

To construct the simplest form of stem-and-leaf display we begin by choosing a suitable pair of adjacent digits in the data—in the IQ example the tens digit and the units digit. Next we split each data value between these two digits. For example the value 99 would be split as follows:

Data Value   Split   stem   and   leaf
99   9/9   9   and   9

Then we allocate a separate line in the display for each possible string of leading digits (the *stem*). Finally we write down the trailing digit (the *leaf*) of each data value on the line corresponding to its leading digit.

Stem-and-Leaf Plot for Child IQ Scores
(All Mothers)

Low : 22 48

```
 8 : 14
 8 : 699
 9 : 2223
 9 : 66899999
10 : 00111223334
10 : 667789
11 : 00001223444
11 : 5556777777778888889999
12 : 01123344444
12 : 5667777789
13 : 4
13 : 99
14 : 14
```

(Two observations are not included in the main stem-and-leaf diagram since they are so far removed from the others. They are however specifically noted before the plot proper).

---

that the group of children whose mothers were depressed is much smaller than the other group?

SIDNEY

Well, a *back-to-back* stem-and-leaf display might be helpful; this is constructed using the same stems for each group and placing the leaves to the left and right. Here such a plot (see Display 2.3) seems to suggest some difference in average IQ of the two groups and perhaps a difference in how the values spread out from this average.

FRANCES

The stem-and-leaf displays certainly give a nice picture of the data, but if I want a more concise summary, do I simply calculate the data's mean and standard deviation?

```
        Display 2.3 Back-to-back Stem-and-leaf Plots for Child IQ Scores for
                     Non-depressed and Depressed Mothers

Low : 22   48

      41 :  8 :  699
         :  9 :  2223
      96 :  9 :  689999
  72110 : 10 :  0123334
         : 10 :  66789
       1 : 11 :  0000223444
         : 11 :  5556777777778888889999
      31 : 12 :  012344444
       9 : 12 :  566777778
         : 13 :  4
       9 : 13 :  9
         : 14 :  14
```

2.3   Numerical and Graphical Summaries of a Data Set

SIDNEY

Well, let's stop and think for a moment what we're actually doing when we report simple summary statistics. The classical summary statistics are the sample mean, and the sample variance, or its square root, the sample standard deviation. You'll remember how we compute them (see Display 2.4).

Now, although these statistics are almost universally used by researchers in psychology and the social sciences, they're not ideal for all data sets. For example, problems can arise if the data set contains a single "wild" or "outlying" value, since this can often considerably affect either the sample mean or the sample variance.

FRANCES

That certainly seems to be the case in this sample. There is one child with an IQ of only 22. I think that child was also diagnosed as suffering from autism, so it's not clear to me whether his score should be included at all.

SIDNEY

We should look at the sample mean and variance for the data including and excluding this child. The mean changes from 110.9 to 111.9, and the variance from 300.7 to 217.3; the latter is a fairly substantial change.

FRANCES

Is there any way around this problem other than simply removing the wild observations—and how do you decide which are the wild observations?

SIDNEY

We can leave the question of identifying outlying observations for the moment, and first consider some alternative summary measures that are *resistant*—an arbitrary change in a small part of the sample can have only a small effect on the summary statistic. These measures are based

---

Display 2.4 Mean and Variance

Assume we have a sample of data that consists of n observations represented by $x_1, x_2, \ldots, x_n$. The classical summary statistics are the *sample mean*, $\bar{x}$ and the *sample variance*, s^2 or its square root, the *sample standard deviation*. The mean is calculated as:

$$\bar{x} = \frac{1}{n} \sum_{i=1}^{n} x_i$$

In other words, one sums all the scores and divides by the number of observations. The mean expresses the sample's *central tendency*.

Also required is a measure of the extent to which the observations group closely around, or spread rather far around, the sample mean. The variance of the sample is calculated as

$$s^2 = \frac{1}{n-1} \sum_{i=1}^{n} (x_i - \bar{x})^2$$

Because the calculation of the variance entails squaring numbers, the result looks quite different from the mean—it's much bigger. To return to the scale of the raw data we take the square root of the variance to get the standard deviation.

The sample mean and variance of a variable can be used to produce *standard scores*, i.e. scores with mean zero and standard deviation one, by the simple transformation

$$z = \frac{x - \bar{x}}{s}$$

---

on *sorting* and *counting* the data (see Display 2.5). Taken together, the median, fourths, and extremes constitute what is often known as *the five-number summary*. Let's have a look at what we get for the IQ data (see Display 2.6).

FRANCES
What are the advantages of this type of summary over the more conventional mean and variance?

SIDNEY
One major advantage is that the median and fourths are resistant to the impact of wild observations—in fact, up to 25% of the data values can be made arbitrarily large ("wild") without greatly disturbing the median or the fourths. Further advantages are that the five-number summary can be used to provide an appealing graphical display known as a *box plot*, which shows much of the structure of the data, and by introducing the idea of the *fourth-spread* we can make the concept of a "wild" observation less vague (see Display 2.7).

Having calculated the five-number summary, construction of a box plot

---

Display 2.5 The Five-number Summary of a Data Set

Firstly the data are sorted into ascending order, which we will represent as

$$x_{(1)}, x_{(2)}, \ldots, x_{(n)}$$

where $x_{(i)}$ represents the i-th *smallest* observation. On the basis of this ordering we can define the *rank* of an observation in either of two ways: we may count up from the smallest value or we may count down from the largest. The first of these yields the observation's *upward rank* and the second its *downward rank*. One further term we need before we can move on to consider possible summary statistics is the *depth* of a data value, which is simply the smaller of its upward and downward rank.

By using the notion of depth it is possible to specify a number of useful summary values which can be easily calculated for a data set. Perhaps the most familiar is the *median*, which gives the centre of the sample in terms of counting. Its depth is $(n + 1)/2$, so that if $n = 3$ then the median is $x_{(2)}$. If n is even, say $n = 2k$, then the median falls halfway between $x_{(k)}$ and $x_{(k+1)}$.

The next two summary statistics can be found extremely simply since they are the two data values of depth 1—in other words the smallest and largest values in the set of observations. Finally to the median and the *extremes* we add another pair of summary values colourfully called the *hinges* or *fourths*, which are defined as values coming halfway between the median and each extreme. The two fourths bracket the middle half of the data.

Taken together the median, fourths and extremes constitute what is often known as the *five-number summary* of a data set.

Display 2.6 Five-number Summaries for Child IQ Scores

Group	L.Ext.	L.Frth	Med.	U.Frth	U.Ext.
All Mothers	22.0	101.0	114.5	121.0	144.0
Non-Depres. Mothers	48.0	103.0	116.0	122.0	144.0
Depres. Mothers	22.0	96.0	101.0	121.0	139.0

---

is very simple (see Display 2.8). Let's see how the box plot looks for the IQ data (see Display 2.9).

FRANCES
I can see that this produces an appealing and informative graphical summary of the data, but couldn't we have constructed a similar plot based on the sample mean and variance?

SIDNEY
Yes, but such a plot would necessarily lack resistance to the influence of even a single wild data value. One further point about the box plot is that our definition of outliers is essentially arbitrary, but experience with

---

Display 2.7 Fourth Spread and Wild Observations

The *fourth-spread*, d_f, is the range of data values defined by the upper(F_u) and lower(F_l) fourths, i.e.

$$d_f = F_u - F_l$$

Cutoffs to define outlying or *wild* observations are taken as $F_l - \frac{3}{2}d_f$ and $F_u + \frac{3}{2}d_f$

For the IQ scores of all the mothers $d_f = 20$ so the cutoff points for defining wild observations are 71 and 151. The children with IQ scores 22 and 48 are therefore considered as outliers.

Display 2.8 Constructing Box Plots

To construct a box plot we first draw a box with ends at the lower and upper fourths and a crossbar at the median. Next we draw a line from each end of the box to the most remote point that is **not** an outlier as defined in Display 4.7. The resulting figure schematically represents the body of the data **minus** the outliers. The outliers can be incorporated into the final diagram individually by representing them as asterisks situated beyond the outlier cutoffs.

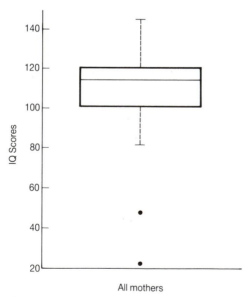

Display 2.9   Box Plot of Child IQ Scores

many data sets suggests that this definition serves us well in identifying those values that may require special attention.

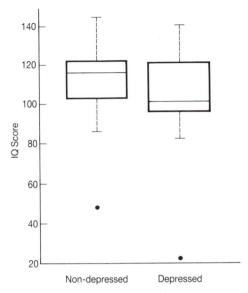

Display 2.10   Box Plots of Child IQ Scores

FRANCES
Would it be useful to construct box plots separately for the IQ scores of children of mothers depressed postnatally and the scores of children whose mothers did not suffer from such depression?

SIDNEY
Certainly, since a display of such *parallel box plots* allows us to compare several batches of data, and to see similarities and differences among the batches. Here a comparison of the two box plots (see Display 2.10) confirms the points noted in our discussion of the stem-and-leaf plots of the two groups.

2.4   Transforming Data

SIDNEY
Once you've examined the raw data by means of a series of stem-and-leaf plots, summary statistics and box plots, it may become apparent that a number of variables in which you're interested do not have satisfactory distributional properties; for example, when you plot the distribution it may depart quite a bit from a normal bell-shaped curve. Many statistical procedures assume that the data conform to a normal distribution and so this could give rise to difficulties in applying routine statistical tests or simple model-fitting procedures such as regression, even when such tests and procedures purport to be "robust" against violations of their own assumptions. There are several reasons why problems might arise. The raw data might have

(a)   strong asymmetry—with many more scores on one side of the distribution than the other;

(b)   several outliers, or "wild" observations;

(c)   samples in different groups or treatment conditions with widely
different spreads.

FRANCES
**I understand the first two of these but would like an example for the last
one.**

SIDNEY
Well, the point about different spreads in different groups is illustrated
by the IQ scores of children of the two types of mothers, postnatally
depressed and not depressed. Both the stem-and-leaf plots and the box
plots indicate clearly that the scores of the former are more widely spread
and this could cause problems in a formal comparison of the two sets of
scores.

FRANCES
So what can I do to deal with these problems?

SIDNEY
Well, by altering the shape of the sample or samples we may often be able
to alleviate the difficulty. Essentially what we try to do is to *transform* the
data by applying a single mathematical function to all the values in the
raw data, so that the transformed values meet the assumptions of our test
procedure more satisfactorily (see Display 2.11). Many functions might
be considered for such transformations but let's content ourselves here
with looking at only those that have been found to be useful in a variety
of different situations. Such transformations all have certain properties in
common:

(a)   *They preserve the order of data in a sample.* Spacing between data
points may change, but the order of values remains the same.

(b)   *They preserve summary statistics of the data that are based on the
order of the sample values.* In particular, medians are transformed to
medians and fourths to fourths.

(c)   *They are continuous functions.* This guarantees that points that are
very close together in the raw data will also be very close together
in the transformed sample, at least relative to the scale being used.

The commonly used transformations form a class known generally as
power transformations (see Emerson and Stoto 1983); the most commonly
used transformations from this class are the *logarithmic* and the *square
root* transformations.

FRANCES
**A variable in this sample that might require a transformation because of
the asymmetry of the raw data is the number of behaviour problems a
child shows at 4 years. A box plot of the observations on this variable (see
Display 2.12) shows some degree of right-skewness.**

Display 2.11 Transformations

A transformation of the sample $x_1, x_2, \ldots, x_n$ is a function T that replaces each x_i by a new value $T(x_i)$ so that the transformed values of the sample are $T(x_1), T(x_2), \ldots, T(x_n)$.

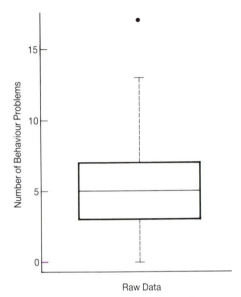

Raw Data

Display 2.12 Number of Behaviour Problems—Box Plot

SIDNEY

Yes, the plot does show that the distribution of this variable is at least a little skew and this might cause problems for future analyses carried out on this variable. Let's see if a log-transformation is any help by constructing a box plot of the log-transformed observations. Since some children have no behaviour problems, and you can't take a log of zero, we will actually take the logs of the number of behaviour problems plus one (see Display 2.13). Now we see that the right-skewness is considerably reduced.

FRANCES

Does this mean that if a variable has a distribution that is highly skew I should always transform it to log scores?

SIDNEY

Not necessarily; often if you're trying to achieve symmetry the choice of transformation may involve applying several rules of thumb:

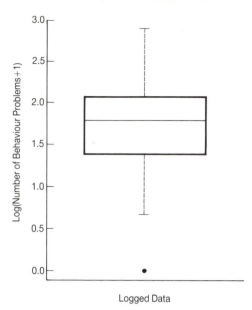

Logged Data

Display 2.13 Log(N. of Behaviour Problems +1)—Box Plot

(a) If it's important to achieve symmetry in the main body of the data, but skewness in the tails is relatively unimportant, the log-transformation is probably preferable.

(b) If considerations of symmetry in the tails of the distribution are important, the square-root transformation might be more appropriate.

(c) If we want to transform in a way that tries to balance the degree of skewness of the main part of the distribution against the more modest skewness in the extremes, we might use the fourth root.

Incidentally, there are some methods available for fine-tuning a transformation so that it more nearly achieves symmetry; these are described in Emerson and Stoto (1983).

FRANCES
What about the other problems you mentioned, beyond asymmetry?

SIDNEY
One important situation is where we wish to compare several groups of individuals. We would like the groups to have approximately equal spreads, this being an assumption made by many methods we might want to apply to the data, such as analysis of variance.

FRANCES
In the sample we're looking at, I would like at some time to compare the IQ scores of the daughters and sons of the depressed and well women. Should we take a look at the distribution of these in each group?

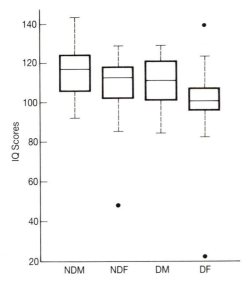

Display 2.14   Box Plots for Four Groups Child IQ Scores—Raw Data (NDM: Non-depressed mothers—male children. NDF: Non-depressed mothers—female children. DM: Depressed mothers—male children. DF: Depressed mothers—female children.)

SIDNEY
Yes, let's construct box plots for each of the four groups (see Display 2.14).

FRANCES
These seem to show that the spread of the observations differs somewhat in the four groups. So we should take a log transformation here?

SIDNEY
Yes, I think that would be useful for a variety of reasons:

(a)   The transformed data will be better suited for comparison and visual exploration.
(b)   The transformed data may be better suited for common statistical analyses. For example, classical one-way analysis of variance models assume constant variance within groups.
(c)   Other benefits may result from the transformation. Individual samples may become more nearly symmetric and have fewer outliers.

In this case, a box plot of the log-transformed scores (see Display 2.15(a)) does look slightly more acceptable. For interest I've also constructed the box plots after a square-root transformation (see Display 2.15(b)).

FRANCES
So transformations can be useful for putting a set of data into "better shape" for later analyses, but can they also be helpful in simplifying further analyses?

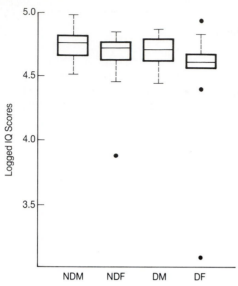

Display 2.15 (a)   Box Plots for Four Groups Child IQ Scores—Logged Data

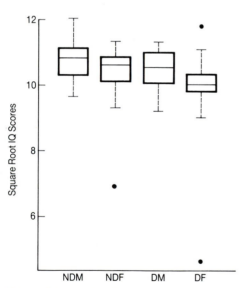

Display 2.15 (b)   Box Plots for Four Groups Child IQ Scores—Square Root Data

SIDNEY

Well, a further common situation in which we might seek a transformation is when we're investigating the relationship between two variables, or deriving an equation relating one variable to another. You'll recall that this is the province of the correlation coefficient and the technique known as regression (see Display 2.16). The aim of a transformation here is generally to make the relationship under investigation simpler, in par-

---

Display 2.16

(a) Correlation

Suppose two variables have been observed on each of *n* individuals giving the pairs of scores $(x_1, y_1), \ldots, (x_n, y_n)$. To quantify the direction and degree of the relationship between the two variables we can use the *correlation coefficient* which is defined as follows:

$$r = \frac{\sum_{i=1}^{n} (x_i - \bar{x})(y_i - \bar{y})}{\sqrt{\sum_{i=1}^{n} (x_i - \bar{x})^2 \sum_{i=1}^{n} (y_i - \bar{y})^2}}$$

r takes values between -1 and 1, with the sign indicating the *direction* of the relationship between *x* and *y* and the magnitude the strength of the relationship. It is important to remember that *r* is a sensible measure *only* when the relationship between the two variables is approximately linear.

(b) Regression

When examining the relationship between a pair of variables, it is sometimes of interest to go beyond simply calculating their correlation and to derive an equation relating the *y* variable to *x*. In the simplest, *linear regression*, case we assume that the equation has the form

$$y_i = a + b(x_i - \bar{x}) + \epsilon_i$$

where the ϵ_i represent the amount that the observed values of *y* deviate from the values predicted by the regression equation. The constants *a* and *b* can be estimated from the *n* pairs of observations as:

$$a = \bar{y}$$

$$b = \frac{\sum_{i=1}^{n} (x_i - \bar{x})(y_i - \bar{x})}{\sum_{i=1}^{n} (x_i - \bar{x})^2}$$

---

ticular, to make it approximately linear. This would have the advantage that simple correlational and regression methods could be applied, so that interpretation of results would become far more straightforward.

As an example, let's examine the IQ scores and behavioural problems in your sample of four-year-old children. The scatter diagram for these data after removing those children with IQ values below 50 (see Display 2.17), shows only a very moderate relationship, the correlation coefficient taking the value -0.183. The negative value indicates that children with lower IQ scores tend to have more behaviour problems although the actual magnitude of the coefficient indicates that this relationship is very weak. What happens if we log-transform the number of behavioural problems? In this case not much! The new scatter diagram (see Display 2.18) seems to suggest an even weaker relationship between the two variables, although the correlation coefficient is basically unchanged. A simple linear regression may be fitted to both the raw and the log-transformed data (see Displays 2.19 and 2.20) and we can see that in each case the line is

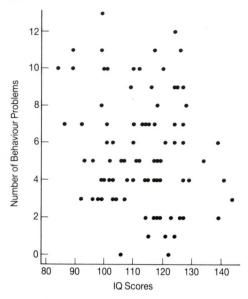

Display 2.17   IQ v N. of Behaviour Problems (Raw Data)

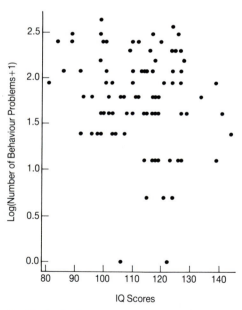

Display 2.18   IQ v Log (N. of Behaviour Problems + 1)

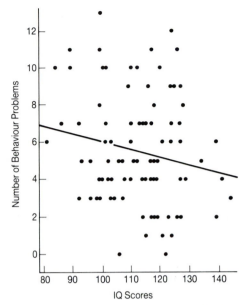

Display 2.19   Regression Line for IQ v N. of Behaviour Problems

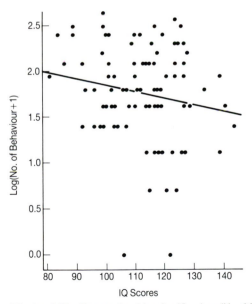

Display 2.20   Regression Line for IQ v Log (N. of Behaviour + 1)

not far from being horizontal. Here a transformation is clearly of little use or interest.

FRANCES

Are there any *disadvantages* in transforming the raw data?

SIDNEY

Yes, transformations, even when they are carried out correctly and bring certain advantages, can also bring disadvantages. With few exceptions a transformation creates a new scale which is often less familiar to the investigator than the original. As a result, it may be harder to understand patterns in the data intuitively, and to make interpretations. For example, for most investigators, it's easier to think of weight in pounds, height in inches or time in months rather than log (pounds), square-root inches, or months squared. So when we are considering whether or not to transform data, we need to ask whether the benefits justify the effort needed and the possible inconvenience that may result in terms of interpretation and communication of findings.

3

Designing and Planning a Study: Hypothesis Testing, Experimental Design and Power Calculations

3.1 Introduction

One of the most difficult tasks any researcher faces is the design and planning of a study. Deciding which measures to take, how to sample subjects, what control procedures to use, whether randomisation is possible, what extraneous sources of variation might be present, how many subjects will be needed, and so forth, can frequently be difficult matters to judge. An inappropriate decision at this stage could easily make the difference between the success or failure of an investigation.

In our fictional example, we shall assume that Frances has sought consultation from the statistician even before applying for funding for the project. (This is after all a fictional example!) Nonetheless, some difficulties still lie ahead. To add to the social realism of our account, the psychologist is working in an area of clinical relevance and no few practical difficulties. Her aim is to learn how to prevent the occurrence of postnatal depression and its associated problems for children.

With this objective in mind, she wishes to conduct an experimental prevention study in a group of women who are particularly at risk of experiencing depression in the first few months after childbirth. Some hypotheses have arisen from her examination of findings from the previous study, as described in Chapter 2. In this chapter, Frances and Sidney now discuss her specific research goals and some possible strategies she might pursue.

3.2   Developing Testable Hypotheses

FRANCES

I'm hoping to conduct a study that is designed to prevent the occurrence of postnatal depression in women who have a prior history of depressive episodes. I have both a short-term and a long-term goal. The short-term goal is to prevent these women from entering into a state of full-blown depression, but also if they do succumb to depression, to help them keep functioning and taking care of their babies whilst they recover from the depressive episode. The long-term goal is to reduce possible problems for their children's development. It's been reported that children's IQ scores are lowered if their mothers are depressed during the first months of life. It's also been suggested that the children of depressed mothers are themselves particularly vulnerable to depression and other psychiatric problems. Thus I want both to observe families during the first six months of the baby's life, during the time when the mothers might be most likely to become depressed, and then again when the child is three years old—when signs of academic and emotional problems might be developing.

SIDNEY

What you seem to be describing so far is a longitudinal study of a population of families who are at risk for particular problems. But you also are talking about a means of *preventing* some of those problems from occurring. What sort of prevention do you have in mind?

FRANCES

General practitioners and the nurses who visit mothers after childbirth and who run well-baby clinics are well aware of the risk of postnatal depression, and probably have a tendency to keep an eye on particular women who, in their view, are particularly at risk for becoming depressed. If they got really worried about a woman, the GP would probably either prescribe anti-depressant medication or refer her for psychiatric care. It's not clear to me, however, whether this general watchfulness will really be effective in preventing the occurrence of depression. My reading of the literature on the subject suggests that the depression in the mother is quite closely associated with marital conflict and the father's own psychiatric problems. I think an effective prevention programme would have to go beyond the ordinary postnatal health visiting and clinics—it would have to involve the father as well. I have designed an intervention programme that involves weekly visits by a child development specialist and fortnightly discussions of marital and family problems with a family therapist. I would like to contrast this approach with the ordinary care offered by the woman's local health authority.

SIDNEY

You certainly seem to have a lot of interesting ideas about how to investigate the problems of postnatal depression, but what I think would be most useful at this stage is to translate these into a small number of specific hypotheses. Would this be possible?

FRANCES

Well, in terms of the previous study whose findings set the context for my research, my starting point is the general hypothesis that, if a mother becomes depressed in the first few months after the birth of a child, that child has an increased likelihood of developing academic and emotional problems. In terms of my specific study, I am hypothesising, first of all, that if a family is given the opportunity to consult with a child develop-ment specialist and a family therapist, the mother is less likely to become depressed. Secondly, I am hypothesising that if a family participates in this prevention programme, the child will be less likely to develop academic and emotional problems later on.

3.3   Experimentation, Randomisation and Control Procedures

SIDNEY
It's worth looking at some of the differences amongst the various hypothe-ses, and the evidence that would be required to test them. You should realise at the outset that what you describe as your starting premise, the hypothesis that the mother's depression affects the child adversely, is the hardest to get to grips with. For example, you say that it has been reported that IQ scores of children of depressed mothers are lower than those of children whose mothers had not been depressed after childbirth. There are at least two possible explanations of that finding:

(a)   Depression in the mother causes a difference in the intellectual de-velopment of the child.
(b)   Some unidentified factor (such as the family's socioeconomic circum-stances) affects both the tendency to depression in the mother and the lower IQ scores of the child.

In other words, some other explanatory factor may be *confounded with* the explanatory factor you have hypothesised to cause the outcome. Much of what we do in designing any study is to try to find ways to minimise the potential influences of confounding factors.

The reason why your second and third hypotheses might be easier to address than the first is because they both involve the use of an *experimental approach*. You'll recall that the main difference between an experiment and a non-experimental study is that the experiment allows the researcher more control, in the sense that particular factors in the study may actually be manipulated. In particular, subjects can be randomly allocated to different groups. Such randomisation serves several functions: it provides an impartial method of allocation free from personal biases, and it ensures a firm basis for the application of significance tests and most of the rest of the statistical methodology likely to be applied to data arising from the study. Most importantly, it distributes the effects of potentially confounding variables, both measured and unobserved, in a statistically acceptable fashion. Random assignment of subjects to groups makes the interpretation of any group differences that emerge relatively unambiguous.

In your proposed study you have hypothesised that a particular in-tervention programme will reduce the incidence of depression. It should be possible to investigate this hypothesis by conducting an experiment in which families are randomly assigned to two groups, one of which receives the experimental prevention programme and the other the ordinary postnatal care provided by the local health authority. Does this seem reasonable?

FRANCES

I can, of course, see the advantages of randomisation and in theory it should be possible. But it does raise both practical and ethical issues. For example, it's been shown that some women are especially likely to be at risk for depression—those who are financially disadvantaged, living in poor housing, possibly with other small children already. These women may need all the help they can get. Is it ethical to assign some of them randomly to the control group of mothers receiving only the normal postnatal care?

SIDNEY

I sympathise, but without random allocation any difference between type of postnatal care will be confounded with the mother's socioeconomic circumstances and vulnerability to depression.

FRANCES

OK, suppose I do manage to assign such women randomly to the experimental prevention programme. They are possibly going to find it very difficult to participate in it, since their lives are already very stressful. Their spouses may be less likely to participate in the family therapy part of the programme. It's possible that very highly stressed families would find the prevention programme much more difficult than the normal care offered by the GP. What if some women, perhaps the most vulnerable to the depression, drop out of the study almost immediately? Then, even though I started out with random assignment, I would end up with groups of quite different women.

SIDNEY

I can see this is a very real problem. My only suggestion, apart from encouraging you to persuade as many women as possible to stay in the study, is to measure not just whether the woman becomes depressed, but also how long she goes without becoming depressed and how long she stays with the prevention programme. I assume this will be possible?

FRANCES

Oh yes. I am planning to visit each of the women every two weeks during the first six months following childbirth, so recording how many weeks they stay well and how many weeks they stay in the programme will be relatively simple. But surely it will be difficult to compare these measures in the two groups because some women will stay well for the whole six months and also because many women hopefully will stay in the trial for six months.

SIDNEY

Fortunately, there are now methods available that will allow meaningful group comparisons despite the problems you have identified. We will talk about them in detail when you have some data.

FRANCES
Well, that's encouraging—perhaps now we could return to the question of my first hypothesis. I can understand the advantages of experimentation, but here the approach is just not a possibility in that we clearly cannot randomly assign some women to become depressed and others to stay healthy and happy. But couldn't we accomplish much the same thing by simply comparing the children of depressed women with those of non-depressed women who have many of the same background characteristics as those who are depressed? In other words, can't we *match* depressed and non-depressed women and then look at their children?

SIDNEY
In general, experiments are the preferred type of study because they are more likely to provide unambiguous results. There are clearly, however, many areas of interest where experiments are simply not possible, and where the researcher is forced to consider other designs. Your investigation of a possible link between depression in mothers and later academic and emotional problems in their children obviously falls into this category. But you will be able to organize a *cohort* (or *prospective*) study in which the children of a group of women who suffer postnatal depression, and those of a group of women who stay well, are followed up over a period of time and their academic performance and emotional well-being measured. In undertaking such a study, matching the mothers on variables considered to be relevant to the academic and emotional development of children may, as you suggest, be very helpful. But clearly matching can only partially overcome the disadvantages of not being able to randomise. Mothers will only be able to be matched on a small number of variables and it is always a possibility that matching on one variable that you know about may result in mismatching on others that you have not specified.

Having said a little about how you might go about collecting information relevant to your first hypothesis, I should like to return once again to the details of your intervention programme, which, as I recall, involves both consultation with a child development specialist and the use of family therapy procedures. Would it be of interest to try to disentangle their effects or are you only concerned with how they perform in combination?

FRANCES
It would be quite helpful if we could say something about their effects separately. What do you have in mind?

SIDNEY
The simplest approach would be to study four rather than just two groups of mothers—one where both prevention techniques are used, one with the child development specialist only, one with family therapy only and one with the usual care offered by the health authority. Each of the treatment groups might be tested against the control group. It might be particularly interesting to try to assess whether using the specialist and family therapy together gave a particular advantage.

FRANCES
I think that would be a good design, as I would be interested in determining the effectiveness of the combined prevention programme versus each alone.

But what shall I do about control procedures? I know that since we are going to use random assignment to form the groups, the effects of possible confounding variables should be distributed roughly equally amongst the groups. But would there be any advantage in attempting to identify particular extraneous variables that might be influencing the mother's likelihood of being depressed—for example, her financial circumstances, her prior history of depression and the degree of conflict she experiences with her husband?

SIDNEY

It might be helpful to include such measures as *covariates* even when the groups are formed by random allocation. If they are strongly related to your dependent variables, then the precision of group comparisons can be improved by including them. The appropriate method is *analysis of covariance*, as we shall see when we start to analyse your data.

FRANCES

A question I haven't asked up to now, but one that I imagine statisticians have to deal with frequently is, how many mothers do I need to study?

3.4   Estimating the Number of Subjects Needed in a Study

SIDNEY

This is often the first, and in some cases the only, question that many researchers put to a statistician. In many cases it is the most difficult of all questions to answer, because it requires some background information that very often the investigator cannot supply. Let me start by answering your question with one of my own. How well do you think you understand the general logic involved in testing an experimental hypothesis?

FRANCES

Quite well, I should imagine. I know that you set up a null hypothesis that the experimental and control groups don't really differ on the variable you're measuring, and that you attempt to reject that null hypothesis. In other words, you're testing a hypothesis that is the opposite of what you really think is going to be true. In my study, for example, I really think that the prevention programme is going to reduce the incidence of depression, compared to standard postnatal care. But what I would be testing in my statistical analysis is the null hypothesis that the prevention programme makes no difference at all and the groups don't differ to any great extent.

SIDNEY

That's fine. But before I talk about sample size, let me give you a little test that a statistician named Oakes (1986) put to 70 academic psychologists:

"Suppose you have a treatment which you suspect may alter performance on a certain task. You compare the means of your control and experimental groups (say 20 subjects in each sample). Further suppose you use a simple independent means t-test and your result is $t = 2.7$, d.f. $= 18$, $p = 0.01$. Please mark each of the statements below as 'true' or 'false.'"

Display 3.1 Frequencies and Percentages of 'True' Responses to Oakes' Test

Statement	f	%
1. The null hypothesis is absolutely disproved	1	1.4
2. The probability of the null hypothesis has been found	25	35.7
3. The experimental hypothesis is absolutely proved	4	5.7
4. The probability of the experimental hypothesis can be deduced	46	65.7
5. The probability that the decision taken is wrong is known	60	85.7
6. A replication has a 0.99 probability of being significant	42	60.0

---

(1)   You have absolutely disproved the null hypothesis (that there is no difference between the population means).

(2)   You have found the possibility of the null hypothesis being true.

(3)   You have absolutely proved your experimental hypothesis (that there is a difference between the population means).

(4)   You can deduce the probability of the experimental hypothesis being true.

(5)   You know, if you decide to reject the null hypothesis, the probability that you are making the wrong decision.

(6)   You have a reliable experimental finding in the sense that if, hypothetically, the experiment were repeated a great number of times, you would obtain a significant result on 99% of occasions."

FRANCES
Well, I sense that you're trying to trick me, and none of the statements sound exactly right, but I guess I would go with Statement 4. I certainly know that in psychological research, we're dealing with probability, not truth.

SIDNEY
You're wrong, but even expressing that level of doubt gets you further than all but 3 of the psychologists Oakes studied. All of the statements are in fact wrong. The correct interpretation is that the p-value expresses the probability of finding a difference between the means as large as, or larger than, the observed difference, assuming that the null hypothesis is true. But look how the psychologists in Oakes' sample responded (Display 3.1).

Only 3 subjects correctly described all six statements as false, and Oakes concluded that the remaining 67 had a less than sound grasp of the conclusions that may properly be drawn from the results of a significance test. This is not particularly encouraging to the statistician, given that the subjects were all university lecturers, research fellows or postgraduate students with at least 2 years' research experience!

FRANCES
Well, I have certainly been put in my place. I shall be less confident in saying I know anything about statistics in the future. But what exactly does this all have to do with my original question—what sample size should I use?

SIDNEY

The statistical theory that underlies the choice of sample size involves the concept of *power*. In the test I just gave you, the probability value expressed the probability of finding a difference between group means of a certain magnitude, given that the null hypothesis is in fact true and the groups are really samples from the same population. But now let's make the opposite assumption. Let's assume that the null hypothesis is indeed false, and ask, what is the power of our experiment? Power is defined as the probability that a statistical test will lead to the rejection of the null hypothesis when the null hypothesis is truly false.

In any particular situation, there are three factors that determine the power of the test:

(1)   the significance level adopted by the experimenter—the decision made beforehand to reject the null hypothesis if the probability of finding such a difference when the null hypothesis was true was 10%, 5%, 1%, or whatever. Conventionally, psychologists tend to adopt a significance level of 5%, but that may vary from situation to situation;

(2)   the reliability of the measurements of the outcome variable;

(3)   the size of the difference between the means of the treatment groups—what we shall call the *effect size*.

Researchers who employ significance tests often give little thought to the power of their tests. Such neglect carries several possible dangers. Most importantly, the researcher is likely to misinterpret non-significant results. Such results may be due to the fact that no effect exists; the null hypothesis really is true. Alternatively, the power of the test may be such that the chance of detecting a true effect, given that it exists, was low.

When you ask about the appropriate sample size, then, the place to start is with a choice of significance level, some information about the measurement of your outcome variable, and a good guess about the size of the difference between the means of your groups that you can expect to see. Given this information, the calculation of the required sample size is often relatively straightforward, although the details depend on the type of response variable and the type of test involved. In many cases you can actually consult a table and read off the sample size that is required. Let's assume that we shall set a significance level of 0.05 for your experiment. What do you already know about the measurement of your outcome variable—for example, what do you know about its variability? And what do you know, on the basis of previous work, about the likely difference between your groups?

FRANCES

In my study, of course, there are two quite different outcome variables. One is the number of women who succumb to postnatal depression. The other is the extent to which the child has problems later in childhood. Maybe we could start by focusing on the latter issue. I shall be measuring the children's IQ when they are three. The IQ of course is a standardised measure, and, according to the norms, the mean is 100 and the standard deviation 16. There have been reports in the literature that the mean IQ of the children of depressed mothers is 10 points lower than the mean IQ of the children of women who did not become ill. So I guess that would mean a possible effect size of 10 points if every woman in the control condition became depressed and every woman in the prevention programme escaped becoming depressed. Since that seems a bit unlikely, maybe we could think about an effect size that is somewhat smaller—say, 8 points? Can we now estimate the sample size I need?

SIDNEY
Here the calculations needed involve a z-test for the difference in the means of the two groups (see Display 3.2).

3.5 Summary of the Experimental Hypotheses and Design

SIDNEY
So we now have some idea of the number of subjects needed for part of your study. There is, of course, much more that we could discuss about the problems of observational and experimental studies but rather than spend time on these I think it would be more productive to summarise the results of our previous discussion in terms of the hypotheses you wish to test and your proposed experimental design.

FRANCES
Yes I think that would be useful.

SIDNEY
You initially set forth three hypotheses, two of which should be amenable to testing through experimental methods. Let's begin by looking at these:

(1) Participation in a prevention programme decreases the likelihood that a woman will become depressed in the first six months following childbirth.
(2) The family's participation in a prevention programme decreases the likelihood that the child will develop subsequent academic and emotional problems.

You also considered it would be of interest to compare two different prevention strategies—consultation about child development and participation in family therapy-type discussions—with ordinary care. Do you have specific hypotheses in mind?

FRANCES
Yes, my interest would be in testing each of the following:

(1) All the experimental treatments would be more effective than ordinary care.
(2) The combined treatment would be more effective than either component of the treatment alone.

Display 3.2 Determining Sample Size

In Frances' example the null hypothesis is that the IQ means of children of depressed and non-depressed mothers are the same, and the alternative hypothesis is that the mean of children of non-depressed mothers is greater than the mean of children of depressed mothers. This may be written more formally as

$$H_0 : \mu_1 = \mu_2$$
$$H_1 : \mu_1 > \mu_2$$

where μ_1 and μ_2 are the population IQ means of children of non-depressed and depressed mothers respectively. Let's assume that the population variance of IQ scores is the same in each group and is known to be $\sigma^2 = 256$. The appropriate test statistic for assessing H_0 is given by

$$z = \frac{\bar{x}_1 - \bar{x}_2}{\sigma} \frac{\sqrt{n}}{\sqrt{2}}$$

where $\bar{x}_1$ and $\bar{x}_2$ are the average IQs in the two groups for the sample of n children taken in both. It is n that we want to determine. The null hypothesis is rejected in favour of the alternative if

$$z > z_\alpha$$

where z_α is the appropriate normal deviate (here where $\alpha = 0.05$, $z_\alpha = 1.64$). This is a *one-tailed test* because of the form of H_1. The type II error, β, is defined to be

$$\beta = Pr(accepting \ H_0/H_1 \ true)$$
$$= Pr(z < z_\alpha/H_1 \ true)$$

If H_1 is true z has a normal distribution with mean given by

$$\mu = \frac{\mu_1 - \mu_2}{\sigma} \frac{\sqrt{n}}{\sqrt{2}}$$

and variance equal to one.   (Continued)

---

(3)   Having some experience with family therapy-type discussion would be more effective than consultation with the child development specialist in reducing the mother's tendency to depression.

(4)   Having some consultation about child development would be more effective than the family therapy-type discussions in reducing the child's subsequent academic problems.

SIDNEY

Well these are very clearly set out. Now I think we should start to think about the particular measurements you will be making throughout the course of this study.

Display 3.2 (continued) Determining Sample Size

Therefore

$$\beta = \Pr(< z_\alpha / z \sim N(\mu, 1))$$

So that

$$\beta = \int_{-\infty}^{z_\alpha - \mu} \frac{1}{\sqrt{2\pi}} \exp(-x^2/2)\, dx$$

We can also write that

$$\beta = \int_{-\infty}^{z_\beta} \frac{1}{\sqrt{2\pi}} \exp(-x^2/2)\, dx$$

Consequently

$$z_\beta = z_\alpha - \mu$$

Therefore

$$\frac{\mu_1 - \mu_2}{\sigma} \frac{\sqrt{n}}{\sqrt{2}} = z_\alpha - z_\beta$$

giving

$$n = \frac{2\sigma^2 (z_\alpha - z_\beta)^2}{(\mu_1 - \mu_2)^2}$$

In Frances' example $\sigma^2 = 256$, $\mu_1 - \mu_2 = 8$, and $z_\alpha = 1.64$. To determine n we now only need to specify β and hence z_β. The type II error β is actually 1-power so specifying what power is required sets the value of β. Suppose Frances demands a power of 90% so that $\beta = 0.1$ and $z_\beta = -1.28$. This leads to a value for n of

$$n = \frac{2 \times 256 \times (1.64 - (-1.28))^2}{8 \times 8}$$

i.e. $n = 68$

4

Measurement, Observer Bias and Reliability

4.1 Introduction

The measurements taken on subjects during the course of an investigation should be objective, precise and reproducible. The appropriate measures vary of course from study to study but in all cases it is most important that decisions about measurements be made before the study begins. In many areas of research, particularly in the behavioural sciences, the observer, interviewer or rater is the most obvious source of measurement error. Reliability studies are, consequently, frequently conducted in order to assess the level of observer variability in the measurement procedures to be used in collecting the data of interest. That such studies are essential is a point clearly made in the following quotation from Fleiss (1986):

> "The most elegant design of a study will not overcome the damage caused by unreliable or imprecise measurement. The requirement that one's data be of high quality is at least as important a component of proper study design as the requirement for randomization, double blinding, controlling where necessary for prognostic factors and so on. Larger sample sizes than otherwise necessary, biased estimates and even biased samples are some of the untoward consequences of unreliable measurements that can be demonstrated."

Reliability refers to the consistency or reproducibility of the result given by an instrument measuring the same object or individual repeatedly under different conditions. Absence of reliability can, as Fleiss has remarked, have serious effects on all types of scientific inquiries and so once again a conversation with a statistician may prove profitable.

4.2   Sources of Information and Scales of Measurement

FRANCES

**I thought I might need some advice about the measures I am planning
to use in my various studies. Let me describe briefly what I'm planning.
First, during the prevention programme the mother's** *mental state* **will be
evaluated every two weeks with a short screening questionnaire; she will
get a score from 1 to 10 in terms of the number of depressive symptoms
she has experienced in the past two weeks. If she has a score greater than
6, she will be given a more extensive clinical interview, and a diagnosis will
be made. This will not be a number but a qualitative judgement—whether
a clinician would classify the woman as depressed or not. The question the
clinician asks is, is this woman a "case" at this particular point in time?**

**All these measurement procedures are quite different from the ones that
are used to measure the construct of** *mother–child interaction.* **I am hypothesising that the impact of the mother's mental state on the child is
mediated by particular changes in the way she interacts with the child—in
particular, the emotional quality of their interactions. I plan to observe
the mothers and their babies twice during the first six months, and record
several bits of information about their interactions. I shall actually time
the duration of their face-to-face interaction within an hour of observation
and I shall rate their emotional closeness on a 7-point scale. In addition,
every 5 minutes, I shall rate whether or not the infant and the mother
are showing two particular emotions—***distress* **(***dysphoria* **on the mother's
part), or** *glee.*

The ways in which I want to measure the other constructs—*the child's
academic potential* **and** *the child's emotional problems*—**are different still.
The first will be done in terms of a standardised IQ test which I shall
administer to the child at the age of four; IQ scores correlate substantially
with actual school performance later on. The second will be done in terms
of a standardised behavioural checklist to be filled out by the mothers,
again when the children are three years old.**

SIDNEY

There are several things we should note about what you've just said.
First of all you will be exploiting different sources of information in
making these measurements: standardised tests, naturalistic observations,
clinicians' judgements, self-report questionnaires and so on.

Secondly you are looking at variables having different scales of measurement. Some for example will be *categorical* variables. That means the
variable assigns individuals to different discrete categories. An example
might be affiliation with a particular political party. Some people will be
Conservative, others Labour voters and, a few, supporters of the Liberal-
Democratic party. The resulting data will be *counts* of the number of
people in each category.

Other variables will have *ordinal* properties. That means scores range
along a continuous dimension such as a 5-point rating scale and the
data collected allow the individuals to be *ranked* with respect to the
attribute. For example, psychiatric patients might be rated with respect to
their anxiety as "no anxiety", "mild anxiety", "moderate anxiety", "severe

anxiety", and "very severe anxiety". Perhaps a few variables will be on an *interval* scale so that the differences between each pair of scale points are exactly equal intervals and so can be compared. Some interval scale variables may in addition have a "true" zero point, in which case they are referred to as *ratio* scale variables.

FRANCES
I assume you mean by a true zero that the variable in question is completely absent. So, for example, if I measured the length of different people's journeys to work in miles, someone who didn't go at all would get a zero score?

SIDNEY
That's right. The important thing to remember is that different scales of measurement call for different approaches to their statistical analysis. Put another way, once you know what your design is, what your hypotheses are and something about the scale of the measurements you will be using, decisions about the appropriate method of analysis become far simpler.

FRANCES
Let me see if I can decide what scale of measurement applies to each of the variables I wish to use in my investigation. My measure of the mother's mental state, in terms of the score derived from the screening questionnaire, seems like a ratio scale—it's a count of 10 possible symptoms and she could be symptom-free. That's a true zero, isn't it? On the other hand, the clinician's diagnosis seems like a categorical variable. Each woman who is being interviewed is assigned to one or the other category—either she's depressed or not. When it comes to the measures of mother–child interaction, the 7-point rating scale is ordinal since it seems to me very unlikely that the psychological distance between "quite close" and "very close" is the same as the distance between "quite distant" and "somewhat distant". But the time they spend interacting is clearly a ratio variable, is it not?

SIDNEY
That's about right. The distinction between ordinal, interval and ratio scales is perhaps unimportant in many practical situations. The main distinction we need to make is that between a continuous dimension and a set of discrete categories. Continuous variables will usually require one approach, categorical variables another.

FRANCES
One of the things I'm obviously concerned about is whether the measures I am planning to use are acceptable ones. The standardised IQ tests have been shown to be reliable and valid in other studies, and so have the full-blown psychiatric interview and the children's behaviour problems checklist—but my screening questionnaire and the observational measures are being used for the first time in this study. How do I go about demonstrating their reliability and, if possible, their validity? What I've done so far is to collect data on two small pilot samples. I have observed 10 mother–infant pairs, using the observational measures I've devised.

Display 4.1 Simple Model for Measurement Error

Let us suppose that x represents the observed value for a particular individual on some measurement of interest. If the observation was made a second time under similar conditions it would almost certainly differ to some degree from the first. A simple model for the observations is to assume that there is an underlying "true" value t, which we are trying to measure, which differs from the observed value by some amount e which we can regard as measurement error. The model can then be represented as

$$x = t + e$$

In the population of subjects, t is assumed to have some distribution with mean μ and variance σ_t^2. The error terms are assumed to vary about a mean of zero with variance σ_e^2. Consequently the variability in the observations is a combination of true score and error variance. A quantity which reflects the relative magnitude of the two components of variance is

$$\frac{\sigma_t^2}{\sigma_t^2 + \sigma_e^2}$$

If all variability is due to the true scores this quantity takes the value 1. As error variance becomes more predominant it approaches zero.

SIDNEY

All of the instruments that you're planning to use present particular issues about their reliability, even the standardised ones. Psychometricians have shown that demonstrating the reliability of an instrument in one sample or population does not guarantee that it will operate in the same way in a new population. For example, postnatal depression may affect women's responses to the children's problems checklist, which may interfere with the reliability of that instrument. If it were standardised on women who were not ill it might not be reliable or valid for the population you were studying. So you may have to think about assessing the reliability of each measure individually, including the standardised ones.

FRANCES

Can you remind me just what reliability means in this context?

SIDNEY

Well, very briefly, the concept arises from the classical test theory for psychological measurements in which observed scores are considered to be a measure of the "true" score plus error. The reliability of a test or measuring instrument is then defined as the ratio of the true score variance to the observed score variance. This ratio can vary between 0 and 1 with higher values indicating more reliable measurements (see Display 4.1).

FRANCES

Is this an idea equivalent to the notion of latent and observed variables? Is the true score a measure of the latent variable we're actually trying to get at?

SIDNEY
That's correct. In fact, it's probably the simplest example of relating an observed to a latent variable.

FRANCES
So how do we actually arrive at a figure for the reliability of a measuring instrument?

SIDNEY
There are many ways in which reliability can be measured and investigated, and the design of a reliability study is nearly always dependent on the context within which the study is being undertaken, what sort of measuring instruments are being used or compared, and what properties or characteristics are being measured. There appear to be three main roles for reliability studies—as an aid to instrument development (including training of interviewers, raters etc.), as an aid to the choice of measuring instrument or to the choice of conditions under which measurements should be made; and as a way of monitoring instrument use (quality control). The big question is often "Is the measuring instrument or technique capable of adequately fulfilling its intended role?"

The simplest design for a study of instrument precision would involve repeated measurement on the same subjects using the same instrument under conditions that remain as stable as possible. Of course, when dealing with measuring instruments that are human raters making measurements on human subjects, the situation is not simple because of the possible confounding effects of memory, and changes in the characteristics being measured. Many more complex designs have therefore been proposed.

4.3   Reliability Measures for Categorical Data

FRANCES
Perhaps we can begin by talking about the observational measures that I have developed. In observational studies, the usual way to deal with reliability is to demonstrate that two independent observers agree about their observations on particular behavioural categories. So, for example, in my study, where observers note whether mothers and babies are distressed or happy in particular time intervals, agreement would generally be measured by the percentage of intervals in which both observers make the same rating. In fact, I've already calculated this measure for some of the pilot sample (see Display 4.2).

SIDNEY
Your measure has the virtue of simplicity and is also readily understood. It is not, however, an adequate measure of agreement since it ignores agreement between the observers that might be due to chance. Let me explain. Suppose each of your observers were simply rating the child's affect for each time interval at random in accordance with their individual biases. We can estimate these individual tendencies by examining an appropriate cross-classification table and noting the marginal values (see Display 4.2). For example, observer 1 would simply rate 25% of the

---

Display 4.2 Percentage Agreement Measure

Summary of data for the infant's results on the affect categorised as distress or glee every 5 minutes. A total of 10 subjects were each observed for an hour.

		Observer 1			
		Neither	Glee	Distress	Total
	Neither	61	0	3	64
Observer 2	Glee	7	12	0	19
	Distress	9	0	28	37
	Total	77	12	31	120

Percentage Agreement $= 100 \times \frac{61+12+28}{120} = 84.2\%$

Display 4.3 Calculating Chance Agreement

Suppose the two observers are rating a categorical variable with r categories, and the totals for observer 1 are

$$X_1, X_2, \ldots, X_r$$

and for observer 2

$$Y_1, Y_2, \ldots, Y_r$$

and the total number of patients rated is N. The estimate of the number of patients on which the observers would agree if they rated at random according to their marginal totals is given by

$$N_c = N \left[\frac{X_1 Y_1}{N^2} + \frac{X_2 Y_2}{N^2} + \cdots + \frac{X_r Y_r}{N^2} \right]$$

so that the proportion of chance agreements, P_c, is given simply by $P_c = N_c/N$.

---

intervals "distressed" and 10% "happy" without regard to the actual behaviour occurring in the interval. Such a procedure would still lead to some agreement between the two observers as judged by your measure of agreement. The chance agreement is however easily calculated (see Display 4.3), and this may be used to produce a *chance-corrected* agreement measure (see Display 4.4). This measure is generally known as a *kappa* coefficient.

FRANCES
I can see the advantages of introducing chance agreement in this way, but how do I judge whether the level of agreement found is acceptable, or whether the agreement for different pairs of observers differs?

Display 4.4 The Kappa Coefficient

If the observed proportion of agreement is P_o and the chance agreement P_c then the statistic kappa is defined as

$$\kappa = \frac{P_o - P_c}{1 - P_c}$$

When there is complete agreement between the two observers, P_o will take the value 1, so that the maximum possible excess over chance agreement is $1 - P_c$; the observed excess over chance agreement is $P_o - P_c$ and kappa is simply the ratio of the two differences.

If there is complete agreement $\kappa = 1$. If observed agreement is greater than chance than $\kappa > 0$. If observed agreement is equal to chance $\kappa = 0$. Finally if the observed agreement is less than chance $\kappa < 0$ with its minimum value depending on the marginal distributions.

For the data in Display 3.2 $P_o = 0.842$ and P_c is obtained as

$$P_c = \left[\frac{64 \times 77}{120^2} + \frac{19 \times 12}{120^2} + \frac{37 \times 31}{120^2} \right] = 0.438$$

so that kappa is given by

$$\kappa = \frac{0.842 - 0.438}{1 - 0.438} = 0.719$$

SIDNEY
The question of what values of kappa constitute good agreement is not as straightforward as it may appear. Some arbitrary "benchmarks" for the evaluation of observed kappas have been given (see Display 4.5) but they are of course largely subjective and not universally agreed. The interpretation of results is really largely dependent upon the uses to which the measurements are to be put. In your particular example, however, the agreement between the raters seems to be excellent and gives no cause for concern.

It would be a simple matter to test whether a kappa value differs significantly from zero, this indicating no agreement beyond chance (see Display 4.6), but such a test is of limited practical interest. More important is the associated confidence interval (see Display 4.6) which gives a range of values in which the true kappa value might lie. (For more information about confidence intervals, see Chapter 5.)

FRANCES
I would also like to assess the reliability of some other measures I take, for example, the total time mothers and babies spend in face-to-face interaction. For such continuous measurements can I simply correlate the two observers' scores?

Display 4.5 Benchmarks for Observed Kappas

Landis and Koch (1977) have given arbitrary "benchmarks" for the evaluation of observed kappa values. These are as follows:

Kappa	Strength of agreement
0.00	Poor
0.01–0.20	Slight
0.21–0.40	Fair
0.41–0.60	Moderate
0.61–0.80	Substantial
0.81–1.00	Almost perfect

Display 4.6 Estimated Variance of Kappa

The large-sample variance of a kappa value is given by

$$V = \frac{1}{N(1 - P_c)^4}[\sum_{i=1}^{r} p_{ii}[(1 - P_c) - (p_{.i} + p_{i.})(1 - P_o)^2]$$

$$+ (1 - P_o)^2 \sum_{i=1}^{r} \sum_{j=1}^{r} p_{ij}(p_{.i} + p_{j.})^2 - (P_o P_c - 2P_c + P_o)^2]$$

where p_{ij} represents the proportion of observations in the ij-th cell of the table of counts of agreements and disagreements for the two observers, and $p_{i.}$ and $p_{.j}$ are row and column marginal proportions.

This is useful in setting confidence intervals for kappa values.

For the data in Display 4.2 this variance takes the value 0.0302 and an approximate 95% confidence interval for κ is (0.361,1.000)

4.4 Measuring Reliability of Quantitative Variables

SIDNEY
By correlating the scores of the two observers I suspect you mean calculating Pearson's product moment correlation coefficient between them?

FRANCES
That's certainly what I was thinking of.

SIDNEY
Unfortunately, the simple correlation coefficient is not a particularly useful method of measuring reliability in most cases. For example, it may take the value *one* even when one observer consistently sees, say, twice as much of some behaviour as another (see Display 4.7).

An alternative measure which is more useful is the *intra-class correlation*. In the case of two raters the value of this particular coefficient depends in

Display 4.7 The Product-moment Correlation as a Measure of Agreement

The product-moment correlation coefficient for the following set of scores given by two observers to 15 patients is 1, despite the fact that observer 2 consistently rates twice as high as observer 1.

Observer 1	Observer 2
1	2
3	6
7	14
5	10
2	4
2	4
1	2
6	12
3	6
4	8
8	16
2	4
1	2
1	2
4	8

part on the corresponding product-moment correlation, but in addition is also dependent on the differences between the means and standard deviations of the two sets of scores (see Display 4.8). The two correlations will only be the same when the means for both raters and their standard deviations are the same. Otherwise, the intra-class correlation will be less than the product-moment coefficient.

FRANCES
How would I calculate the intra-class correlation?

SIDNEY
For two raters, the calculation is very simple (see Display 4.9). But the intra-class correlation is also commonly used in situations where more than two raters are involved. In such cases it is calculated via various terms from a two-way analysis of variance of the scores for subjects and raters (see Display 4.9—more about analysis of variance in Chapter 6).

FRANCES
Can I use the same approach for the ratings I have of emotional closeness?

4.5   Measure of Agreement for Ranked Data

SIDNEY
By assigning scores, say 1 to 7, for the various categories of emotional closeness you could use the intra-class measure. But as we discussed

Display 4.8 The Intra-class Correlation Coefficient

In the case of two observers suppose the product moment correlation between their scores is r, then the intra-class correlation r_i is given by

$$r_i = \frac{[\sum(s_1^2 + s_2^2) - (s_1 - s_2)^2]r - (\bar{x}_1 - \bar{x}_2)^2/2}{(s_1^2 + s_2^2) + (\bar{x}_1 - \bar{x}_2)^2/2}$$

where $\bar{x}_1$ and $\bar{x}_2$ are the mean values for observer 1 and observer 2 respectively and s_1 and s_2 the corresponding standard deviations.

For the 10 mother–infant pairs the two observers scores for total time spent in face-to-face interaction are as follows;

Pair	Observer 1	Observer 2
1	15	23
2	40	45
3	17	19
4	35	28
5	13	9
6	40	38
7	54	51
8	21	20
9	30	36
10	35	27

The various terms needed for calculating the intra-class correlation coefficient are as follows:

Mean Observer 1 = 30.0, Variance Observer 1 = 176.67

Mean Observer 2 = 29.6, Variance Observer 2 = 165.38

Correlation between observers scores = 0.913

The value of the intra-class correlation coefficient is 0.912. In this case this is very close to the value of the simple product moment coefficient since the means and variances of the two observers are very similar.

previously what you really have in this case is an ordinal rather than an interval scale and for such measures it is generally advisable to use only the information in the ranked data, since any set of scores assigned to the categories are essentially arbitrary. Agreement between the observers would now be in terms of how their ranked observations conform. For example, if mother–infant pair A has a higher emotional closeness score than mother–infant pair B according to the first observer and is also higher than pair B according to the second observer, there is agreement between the observers on the relative ranks of the two mothers. Disagreement between the two judges occurs when one of them ranks pair A as having greater emotional closeness than pair B and the other ranks pair B as higher than pair A.

Display 4.9 Alternative Calculation of the Intra-class Correlation

The intra-class correlation coefficient for two observers having N scores X_{i1} and X_{i2} is equivalent to Pearson's product moment correlation between $2N$ pairs of observations, the first N of which are the original observations and the second N the same observations with X_{i1} replacing X_{i2} and vice versa.

In the case of more than two raters, the intra-class correlation is calculated from the various terms in a two-way analysis of variance for raters × subjects. If we denote the raters mean square as RMS, the patients mean square as PMS and the error mean square as EMS, and suppose there are N subjects and r raters, then the intra-class correlation is given by

$$r_i = \frac{N(PMS - EMS)}{NPMS + rRMS + (Nr - N - r)EMS}$$

FRANCES
So are there agreement measurements which use only the rank information?

SIDNEY
There are in fact quite a number. Perhaps the simplest is Kendall's rank correlation coefficient. Let's see how this works on your ratings of emotional closeness (see Display 4.10).

FRANCES
The coefficient looks rather low. Perhaps the observers need more training on how to rate this measure or the measure needs to be defined more carefully. Can we now return to your recommendation that I assess the reliability of standardised measures such as the IQ test or the behavioural problems checklist as they are applied in my study. I had thought about selecting a subsample of families and using them to demonstrate the reliability of the instruments in the study as a whole. If I did that, what sorts of reliability assessments should I make?

SIDNEY
One characteristic of many behavioural measurements that distinguishes them from physical measurements is that they are obtained from the responses to several different questions or test items. Your measure of IQ, for example, is probably calculated from answers to several individual tests of cognitive ability.

FRANCES
That's correct.

SIDNEY
One traditional way of obtaining the reliability of a psychological measurement is to split the test into two equal-sized groups of comparable items and to estimate the reliability of the total test score from the subtotals obtained from the two halves. The usual coefficient calculated is *Cronbach's alpha* which can be thought of as a measure of the *internal consistency* of a psychometric test.

Display 4.10 Kendall's Rank Correlation Coefficient

To obtain τ we first obtain the number of pairs of subjects which are ranked in the same order by the two observers—let this equal P. Similarly, let Q be the number of subjects in which the rankings are in the opposite order. Then τ is defined as

$$\tau = \frac{P - Q}{\frac{1}{2}N(N - 1)}$$

When there are tied observations they are given the average of the ranks they would have received if there were no ties. The effect of ties is to modify the formula for τ, which now becomes

$$\tau = \frac{P - Q}{\sqrt{(\frac{1}{2}N(N - 1) - T_A)}\sqrt{(\frac{1}{2}N(N - 1) - T_B)}}$$

where $T_A = \frac{1}{2}\sum_i t_i(t_i - 1)$, t_i being the number of tied observations on the i-th group of ties of Observer A; and $T_B = \frac{1}{2}\sum_j t_j(t_j - 1)$, t_j being the number of tied observations in the j-th group of ties for observer B.

For the 10 mother–infant pairs in the pilot study the observers ratings of emotional closeness were as follows;

Pair	Observer 1	Observer 2
1	5	4
2	6	7
3	4	3
4	5	5
5	3	4
6	6	5
7	7	7
8	6	6
9	4	6
10	3	7

Kendall's τ takes the value 0.33; this is rather low and indicates that ratings of emotional closeness may need to be looked at before the variable is used in the main study.

Another approach would be to simply measure IQ on two occasions separated by two weeks or so and correlate the scores obtained. This is usually known as *test–retest reliability*.

Assessing the reliability of measurements is a large and complex area— an excellent account is given in the book by Dr. Graham Dunn (Dunn, 1989).

5

Comparing Two Groups: the t-test, Mann–Whitney U and Hotelling's T²

5.1   Introduction

For many social and behavioural scientists the *raison d'être* of the statistician is still, it appears, to perform, after the data have been collected, various standard calculations and deliver the verdict *significant* or *non-significant*. The more enlightened among such scientists may also accept that the statistician can be useful in the design and planning stage of a study (Frances is, of course, one of the enlightened) but even a substantial proportion of this group probably still regard the performance of statistical significance tests as a statistician's major contribution to a piece of "collaborative" research. Whether such apparently undiminished enthusiasm for the ubiquitous significance test is entirely justified will be one of the topics of concern in this chapter. Additionally, Frances and Sidney will discuss the assumptions underlying the *t*-test and the construction of confidence intervals.

FRANCES
I'm still keen to sort out what conclusions can be confidently drawn from the earlier study. The first thing I thought I'd look at is the children's IQ scores and compare them in terms of whether or not their mothers had been depressed when the children were three months old. I assume that what I need to do is a simple *independent means t*-test. Am I right?

5.2   The Independent Means *t*-test

SIDNEY
Certainly the *t*-test is often used to compare two groups in the sense of

testing the equality or otherwise of the population means, so it *may* be the test you need. But before calculating the appropriate test statistic and considering possible alternative procedures, perhaps I should begin by reminding you of the assumptions underlying the test:

(a)   Observations are *independent* of one another.
(b)   The variable under investigation (in this case IQ) is normally distributed in both populations.
(c)   The two population variances are equal.

Let's consider each of these in turn with respect to your IQ scores.

(1)   Are the observations independent? Well, there seems to be little reason why this should not be so since there is no apparent mechanism by which one child's score could influence another's. This would not be the case of course, if, for example, several children had been taken from each family, or if the children had been *matched* in some way.
(2)   Are the observations normally distributed? Here the results of our preliminary investigation of the data help (see Chapter 2); they suggest that the data are *not* markedly non-normal, although two of the observations were identified as outliers, and we need to consider carefully whether or not these particular observations should be included in our analyses.
        In general, moderate non-normality can usually be ignored when applying a *t*-test, since the test is known to be relatively *robust* against departures from the normality assumption—essentially this means that derived significance levels will not be too badly affected by such departures. But the robustness property should certainly *not* be taken as justification for applying the *t*-test to data sets irrespective of the shapes of their distributions.
(3)   Are the population variances equal? If we examine the box plots produced for these data (see Display 2.10), we see that there is an indication that the variance of IQ scores for children of depressed mothers is somewhat larger than that for the children of non-depressed mothers. Now there is considerable evidence that the *t*-test is also robust against the *homogeneity* assumption, but less so when the two sample sizes are very different, as they are here, than when they are similar to one another. Consequently, the observed difference in variances may cause some problems. For the moment, however, let's assume that the conditions for a valid *t*-test are met, and go ahead and perform the test using *all* the data (see Display 5.1).

We see that the test statistic has an associated probability of 0.02 and so the conclusion appears to be that the mean IQ scores of children of depressed and non-depressed mothers differ. However, before taking this finding at face value, I think it would be wise to repeat the analysis after leaving out the two "wild" observations previously identified (see Display 5.2). We now find that the sample variances are very similar and

---

Display 5.1 *t*-test for Difference in IQ Scores of Children of Depressed and Non-depressed mothers

Form of the Test

$$H_0 : \mu_1 = \mu_2$$

Group 1:

Number of observations$= n_1$
    sample mean$= \bar{x}_1$
    sample variance$= s_1^2$

Group 2:

Number of observations$= n_2$
    sample mean$= \bar{x}_2$
    sample variance$= s_2^2$

Test-statistic

$$t = \frac{\bar{x}_1 - \bar{x}_2}{s\sqrt{\frac{1}{n_1} + \frac{1}{n_2}}}$$

where

$$s = \sqrt{\frac{(n_1 - 1)s_1^2 + (n_2 - 1)s_2^2}{n_1 + n_2 - 2}}$$

For the IQ data the relevant sample values are

Non-depressed Mothers

$$n_1 = 79, \ \bar{x}_1 = 112.78, \ s_1^2 = 205.50$$

Depressed Mothers

$$n_2 = 15, \ \bar{x}_2 = 101.07, \ s_2^2 = 729.21$$

so that

$$t = 2.46, \ \text{d.f} = 92, \ p = 0.02$$

---

that the more acceptable *t*-test produces much less evidence that the mean IQ scores of the two groups of mothers differ.

FRANCES
That's interesting but also confusing—which result should I report, or should I report both?

SIDNEY
In this case because one outlier has already been identified as representing autistic children (see Chapter 2), and the other may similarly have been mentally handicapped since birth, I think it is legitimate to drop their IQ scores from the group comparison.

Display 5.2 *t*-test for Difference in IQ Scores of Children of Depressed and Non-depressed Mothers after Removing Children with IQs Less than 50

New Sample Values for Depressed Group

$$n_1 = 78, \ \bar{x}_1 = 113.61, \ s_1^2 = 152.97$$

New Sample Values for Non-depressed Group

$$n_2 = 14, \ \bar{x}_2 = 106.71, \ s_2^2 = 270.06$$

New test statistic

$$t = 1.82, \ \text{d.f} = 90, \ p = 0.07$$

FRANCES
Which leads us to conclude that the data provide no evidence that the average IQ scores of children of depressed and non-depressed mothers differ?

SIDNEY
Yes, that's correct, but rather than simply reporting the result of a significance test and its associated *p* value, it is generally much more informative to give an estimate of the size of the group difference and a *confidence interval*.

5.3   Confidence Intervals

FRANCES
What are the advantages of reporting a confidence interval rather than simply the results of a significance test?

SIDNEY
Confidence intervals tell us much more than *p*-values. Even precise *p*-values convey nothing about the size of a group difference. Presenting *p*-values can lead to their being given more merit than they deserve. In particular, there is a tendency to equate *statistical* significance with psychological or clinical importance. But small differences can be statistically significant with large sample sizes, whereas clinically important effects may be statistically non-significant because the number of subjects studied was small.

Confidence intervals on the other hand present a range of values on the basis of the sample data, in which the population value for a group difference may lie. More exactly the confidence interval implies that if a series of identical studies was carried out repeatedly on different samples from the same population and a 95% confidence interval for the group difference calculated in each study, then in the long run 95% of these intervals would be expected to include the population group difference. The effect of small sample size or increased sampling variation will be reflected by an increase in the size of the interval. In essence,

---

Display 5.3 Confidence Intervals for Differences Between Means

The 100(1-α)% confidence interval for the difference in the two population means is

$$\bar{x}_1 - \bar{x}_2 - \left(t_{1-\frac{\alpha}{2}} \times s\sqrt{\frac{1}{n_1} + \frac{1}{n_2}}\right) \text{ to } \bar{x}_1 - \bar{x}_2 + \left(t_{1-\frac{\alpha}{2}} \times s\sqrt{\frac{1}{n_1} + \frac{1}{n_2}}\right)$$

(a) 95% Confidence Interval Based on All Data

$$CI = 2.24 \text{ to } 21.18$$

(b) 95% Confidence Interval Based on Data after Removal of Outliers

$$CI = -0.62 \text{ to } 14.42$$

---

the significance test relates to what a population parameter is *not*; the confidence interval gives a plausible range for what the parameter *is*.

For your IQ scores an estimate of the group difference and a confidence interval are easily calculated (see Display 5.3). Using all the data gives an interval which does *not* include the value zero, consistent with the significant result from the *t*-test. After excluding both the mentally handicapped children the interval includes the value zero, which is the value specified by the null hypothesis in the *t*-test, a hypothesis not rejected for the data without the outliers.

FRANCES
Well, you've convinced me about the advantages of reporting a confidence interval, but I'm still not entirely happy about excluding the outliers. I can see that their inclusion distorts the group comparison when applying the usual form of the *t*-test, but is there no way of obtaining a valid comparison without removing the two observations?

SIDNEY
One possibility might be to perform a version of the *t*-test that does *not* assume that the population variances of the two groups of mothers are equal; another would be to apply a *non-parametric* test such as the *Mann–Whitney*, which since it uses only the *ranks* of the observations will not be so badly affected by the presence of outliers as is the usual *t*-test. Let's have a look at the results from both these procedures (see Display 5.4).

FRANCES
Both seem to confirm the lack of a difference between the IQ scores of the two groups of children although the Mann–Whitney statistic is very close to being significant at the 5% level. I have a question about the Mann–Whitney test. Since it is based on fewer assumptions than the *t*-test, why isn't it always used?

SIDNEY
Well, if the conditions for a valid *t*-test—independence, normality and homogeneity—are all met, then the non-parametric equivalent is less

---

Display 5.4 Alternatives to the Usual *t*-test

(1)   *t-test not assuming homogeneity*

$$t = \frac{\bar{x}_1 - \bar{x}_2}{\sqrt{\frac{s_1^2}{n_1} + \frac{s_2^2}{n_2}}}$$

The approximate degrees of freedom of the test is

$$\text{d.f.} = \frac{1}{\frac{c^2}{n_1-1} + \frac{(1-c)^2}{n_2-1}}$$

where

$$c = \frac{\frac{s_1^2}{n_1}}{\left(\frac{s_1^2}{n_1} + \frac{s_2^2}{n_2}\right)}$$

For *all* the IQ data this version of the test takes the value 1.64 with d.f. = 15.51 The associated probability is 0.12.

(2)   *The Mann–Whitney non-parametric test*

The test statistic, U, is defined as the smaller of U_1 and U_2 where

$$U_1 = n_1 n_2 + \frac{n_1(n_1 + 1)}{2} - R_1$$

$$U_2 = n_1 n_2 + \frac{n_2(n_2 + 1)}{2} - R_2$$

and

n_1=number of observations in group 1

n_2=number of observations in group 2

R_1=sum of ranks assigned to group 1

R_2=sum of ranks assigned to group 2

For moderate to large values of n_1 and n_2 the distribution of the test statistic is approximately normal with mean and variance given by

$$\mu_U = \frac{n_1 n_2}{2}$$

$$\sigma_U^2 = \frac{n_1 n_2 (n_1 + n_2 + 1)}{12}$$

Consequently a normal deviate, z, can be used to test the hypothesis where

$$z = \frac{U - \mu_U}{\sigma_U}$$

For *all* the 94 score on children's IQ the rank sums are

non-depressed mothers, R_1=3936.5,

depressed mothers, R_2=528.5

and the test statistic U takes the value 776.5 with associated p value of 0.06.

powerful. In other words the t-test will more often reject the null hypothesis when it is false. But the difference in power, even in this ideal case, is actually quite small, and non-parametric tests in general, and the Mann–Whitney test in particular, are really quite efficient.

One problem with non-parametric tests is that the appropriate procedures are simply not available for other than relatively simple experimental designs. In many situations, of course, the use of a non-parametric method is unlikely to result in a conclusion that is materially different from that of its parametric equivalent.

FRANCES
After looking at the comparison of the groups with respect to overall IQ, I realised that I hadn't yet investigated my original hypothesis, namely, that the experience of having a depressed mother in infancy would affect some abilities and not others. I believe the mother's depression in infancy might interfere most of all with those abilities that are developing in infancy and less so with verbal and quantitative abilities that develop later. The IQ score we used is actually derived from three sub-scales, *perceptual, verbal* and *quantitative* abilities. Should I look at the comparison of the two groups on each of these scales separately?

5.4   Hotelling's T^2

SIDNEY
Certainly if you are interested in each variable in its own right then a group comparison on each would be appropriate. One would, of course, begin by examining box plots of each separate variable (see Display 5.5), to check distributional assumptions and then if satisfied that all was in order calculate the appropriate test statistics and confidence intervals. Here the only problem appears to be evidence of a number of outliers but for the moment let's keep all the data and perform the usual t-tests and find a confidence interval for the difference between non-depressed and depressed mothers on each variable (see Display 5.6).

FRANCES
The results seem to indicate that there is a difference on the perceptual scale but not on either of the quantitative or verbal scales.

SIDNEY
There is a problem with this approach, namely, that if one carries out a number of tests of true null hypotheses, each at a specified significance level, then the overall probability of incorrectly rejecting one or more of the hypotheses is greater than that specified by the significance level. Indeed, depending on the number of such tests, the overall level can be arbitrarily large (see Display 5.7). The dilemma introduced is that, if we control the probability of rejecting the null hypothesis falsely in each component tests at a conventional level (say 5%), then the overall probability of error is large. On the other hand, to restrict the overall probability to a conventional level we need to make the individual probability levels of the component tests very small (see Display 5.8).

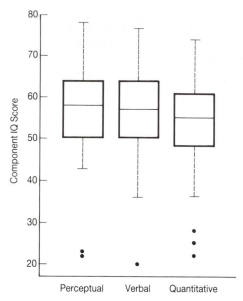

Display 5.5   Box Plots of Component IQ Scores

FRANCES
Suppose now that I was *not* particularly interested in the separate variables but only in the question "Does the set of variables as a whole indicate any between-group differences?" Has this been answered by analysing the overall IQ score derived from the component variables according to a psychometric formula or is there some more appropriate method?

SIDNEY
The problem with simply summing the scores or using an *a priori* formula is that no account is taken of their possible lack of independence. A more satisfactory approach to answering the overall question would be to use Hotelling's T^2.

FRANCES
Is this a *multivariate test procedure*?

SIDNEY
Yes, it's actually the simplest of such procedures and is the multivariate analogue of the two-sample t-test we used earlier. It is appropriate for testing the equality of a whole set of group means—these are usually known as *mean vectors*. A vector is a row of scores on more than one variable—here a row of three scores on the three subtests. In this case, the test assumes that the variances of corresponding variables are the same in both groups and, in addition, that the *covariances* between each pair of variables in each group are equal. In other words, it assumes that the *covariance matrices* of the two groups are the same.

Display 5.6 *t*-tests and Confidence Intervals for Components of IQ

(1)   *Perceptual and Performance Scale* (P)
Non-depressed Group

$$n_1 = 79, \ \bar{x}_1 = 58.27, \ s_1 = 8.78$$

Depressed Group

$$n_2 = 15, \ \bar{x}_2 = 50.93, \ s_2 = 11.38$$

$$t = 2.36, \ 92\text{d.f.}, \ p = 0.03 \quad 95\%\text{C.I.} = 2.08 \text{ to } 12.40$$

(2)   *Verbal Scale* (V)
Non-depressed Group

$$n_1 = 79, \ \bar{x}_1 = 57.14, \ s_1 = 9.87$$

Depressed Group

$$n_2 = 15, \ \bar{x}_2 = 54.80, \ s_2 = 10.50$$

$$t = 0.83, \ 92\text{d.f.}, \ p = 0.41 \quad 95\%\text{C.I.} = -3.24 \text{ to } 7.92$$

(3)   *Quantitative Scale* (Q)
Non-depressed Group

$$n_1 = 79, \ \bar{x}_1 = 55.33, \ s_1 = 9.08$$

Depressed Group

$$n_2 = 15, \ \bar{x}_2 = 51.87, \ s_2 = 11.38$$

$$t = 1.30, \ 92d.f., \ p = 0.20, \quad 95\%\text{C.I.} = -1.83 \text{ to } 8.76$$

FRANCES
Could you just remind me how the covariance is computed and what a covariance matrix might look like?

SIDNEY
The covariance of two variables is calculated a little like the correlation coefficient (see Display 5.9). A covariance matrix is simply the collection of covariances of each pair of variables of interest and their variances arranged in a particular way (see Display 5.9).

FRANCES
Returning to the multivariate analogue of the *t*-test, won't the results of such a test simply reflect those of a series of separate univariate tests? If no differences are found by the separate *t*-tests, then Hotelling's T^2 will lead to the conclusion that the mean vectors of the two groups don't differ,

Display 5.7 Repeated Significance Tests

Number of Repeated Tests at 5% Level	Overall Significance Level
1	0.05
2	0.08
3	0.11
4	0.13
5	0.14
10	0.19
20	0.25
50	0.32
100	0.37
1000	0.53
∞	1.00

Display 5.8 Nominal Significance Levels Required for Repeated Two-sided Significance Tests with Overall Significance Level $\alpha = 0.05$ or 0.01 and Various Values of N, the Maximum Number of Tests

N	$\alpha = 0.05$	$\alpha = 0.01$
2	0.029	0.0056
3	0.022	0.0041
4	0.018	0.0033
5	0.016	0.0028
10	0.0106	0.0018
15	0.0086	0.0015
20	0.0075	0.0013

whereas if any significant difference is found for the component variables, the T^2 statistic will also be significant, right?

SIDNEY

No, that is not necessarily the case; it is possible to have no significant differences for each variable tested separately but a significant T^2 value, and vice versa. This is illustrated most simply by considering two variables and drawing a diagram (see Display 5.10). In a situation such as this it is quite possible that the separate *t*-tests on each variable are both significant whereas a test of whether the *two-dimensional* means of each group differ is likely to be non-significant. The apparently contradictory results are accounted for by the strong correlation between the two variables. When this is allowed for, there is considerable overlap between the two groups.

Display 5.9 Covariance Matrices

The covariance between two variables is estimated from a sample of n pairs of values $(x_1, y_1), (x_2, y_2), \ldots, (x_n, y_n)$ as follows:

$$\text{Cov}(x, y) = \sum_{i=1}^{n} (x_i - \bar{x})(y_i - \bar{y})$$

The variances and covariances of a set of variables, say p, in number can be conveniently arranged in the form of a *matrix*, which is simply a rectangular arrangement of numbers. A covariance matrix for p variables is a $p \times p$ (i.e. one with p rows and p columns), symmetric (i.e. corresponding elements either side of the main diagonal are equal) matrix with variances on the main diagonal and covariances as off-diagonal elements.

$$\mathbf{S} = \begin{pmatrix} \text{Var}(x_1) & \text{Cov}(x_1, x_2) & \cdots & \text{Cov}(x_1, x_p) \\ \text{Cov}(x_2, x_1) & \text{Var}(x_2) & \cdots & \text{Cov}(x_2, x_p) \\ \vdots & \vdots & \vdots & \vdots \\ \text{Cov}(x_p, x_1) & \cdots & \cdots & \text{Var}(x_p) \end{pmatrix}$$

For your data the use of Hotelling's T^2 statistic (see Display 5.11(a)) indicates a significant difference between the two groups.

FRANCES
Is there a multivariate equivalent to finding confidence intervals?

SIDNEY
There is, but it's a little complicated. What can be found is usually referred to as a *simultaneous confidence region* (see Display 5.12). Again the difference from those intervals produced by considering each variable separately is that covariances between variables are allowed for and the size of these affects the size of the confidence interval.

I've calculated the appropriate simultaneous confidence region for the difference in means of the two groups on the perceptual (P), verbal (V) and quantitative (Q) scores; the intervals are quite a bit different from those calculated separately.

FRANCES
In this case the intervals for each variable cover zero but Hotelling's T^2 test gave a significant result. Can this be correct?

SIDNEY
That's an interesting point. In general, when the hypothesis of the equality of the two mean vectors is rejected, at least one of the associated confidence intervals excludes zero. It is not necessary, however, that this is one corresponding to the weight vectors **a**, having a single element equal to one and all others equal to zero—i.e. the vectors we have looked at.

Display 5.10

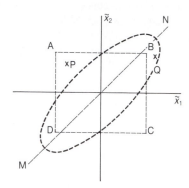

Plot of sample means for a bivariate sample, with regions
within which the hypothesis μ = 0 would not be rejected
when using (1) a multivariate criterion and
(2) two univariate criteria

Suppose we have a sample of n observations on two variables x_1 and x_2, and we wish to test the null hypothesis that $[\mu_1, \mu_2] = [0, 0]$. If we test separately whether each mean takes the value zero then we would use two t-tests. For example to test $\mu_1 = 0$ against $\mu_1 \neq 0$ the appropriate test statistic is $t = \frac{(\bar{x}_1 - 0)}{s_1/\sqrt{n}}$. The hypothesis $\mu_1 = 0$ would be rejected at the α per cent level of significance if $t < -t_{\frac{1}{2}\alpha}$ or $t > t_{\frac{1}{2}\alpha}$, i.e. if $\bar{x}_1$ fell outside the interval $(-s_1 t_{\frac{1}{2}\alpha}/\sqrt{n}, s_1 t_{\frac{1}{2}\alpha}\sqrt{n})$ where $t_{\frac{1}{2}\alpha}$ is the $100(1 - \frac{1}{2}\alpha)$ per cent point of the t-distribution on $(n - 1)$ degrees of freedom. Thus the hypothesis would *not* be rejected if $\bar{x}_1$ fell *within* this interval. Similarly, the hypothesis $\mu_2 = 0$ for the variable x_2 would not be rejected if the mean, $\bar{x}_2$ of the x_2 observations fell within a corresponding interval with s_2 substituted for s_1. The multivariate hypothesis $[\mu_1, \mu_2] = [0, 0]$ would therefore not be rejected if both these conditions were satisfied. If we were to plot the point $(\bar{x}_1, \bar{x}_2)$ against rectangular axes, the area within which the point could lie and the multivariate hypothesis not rejected is given by the rectangle ABCD of the diagram where AB and DC are of length $2s_1 t_{\frac{1}{2}\alpha}/\sqrt{n}$ while AD and BC are of length $2s_2 t_{\frac{1}{2}\alpha}/\sqrt{n}$.

Thus a sample that gave the means $(\bar{x}_1, \bar{x}_2)$ represented by point P would lead to acceptance of the multivariate hypothesis. Suppose, however, that the variables x_1 and x_2 are moderately highly correlated. Then all points (x_1, x_2) and hence $(\bar{x}_1, \bar{x}_2)$ should lie reasonably close to the straight line MN through the origin marked on the diagram. Hence samples consistent with the multivariate hypothesis should be represented by points $(\bar{x}_1, \bar{x}_2)$ which lie within a region encompassing the line MN. When we take account of the nature of variation of bivariate normal samples that include correlation, this region can be shown to be an ellipse such as that marked on the diagram. The point P is *not* consistent with this region and in fact the multivariate hypothesis should be rejected for this sample.   (Continued)

Display 5.10 (continued)

Thus the inference drawn from the two separate univariate tests conflicts with the one drawn from a single multivariate test, and is the wrong inference. A sample giving the $(\bar{x}_1, \bar{x}_2)$ values represented by the point Q would give the other type of mistake, where the two univariate tests lead to rejection of the null hypothesis but the correct multivariate inference is that the hypothesis should not be rejected.

(Reproduced with permission from Krzanowski, 1988).

Display 5.11 Hotelling's T^2 Test

The test statistic T^2 is given by

$$T^2 = \frac{D^2}{\left(\frac{1}{n_1} + \frac{1}{n_2}\right)}$$

where D^2 is the *Mahalanobis distance* between the two groups and is given by

$$D^2 = (\bar{\mathbf{x}}_1 - \bar{\mathbf{x}}_2)' \mathbf{S}^{-1} (\bar{\mathbf{x}}_1 - \bar{\mathbf{x}}_2)$$

and $\bar{\mathbf{x}}_1$ and $\bar{\mathbf{x}}_2$ are the mean *vectors* in each group and $\mathbf{S}$ is the estimate of the assumed common covariance matrix

$$\mathbf{S} = \frac{(n_1 - 1)\mathbf{S}_1 + (n_2 - 1)\mathbf{S}_2}{(n_1 + n_2 - 2)}$$

Under the null hypothesis that the two groups have the same population mean vector

$$F = \frac{(n_1 + n_2 - p - 1)}{(n_1 + n_2 - 2)p} T^2$$

has a Fisher's F-distribution with p and $n_1 + n_2 - p - 1$ degrees of freedom—p is the number of variables.

For the components of IQ data

$$\mathbf{S}_1 = \begin{pmatrix} 77.09 & & \\ 45.74 & 97.53 & \\ 45.74 & 61.47 & 82.48 \end{pmatrix}$$

$$\mathbf{S}_2 = \begin{pmatrix} 129.63 & & \\ 73.41 & 110.31 & \\ 114.92 & 78.83 & 129.55 \end{pmatrix}$$

$$\mathbf{S} = \begin{pmatrix} 85.08 & & \\ 49.95 & 99.47 & \\ 56.27 & 64.11 & 89.64 \end{pmatrix}$$

$$\bar{\mathbf{x}}_1 = [58.26, 57.14, 55.33]$$

$$\bar{\mathbf{x}}_2 = [50.93, 54.80, 51.87]$$

so that $D^2 = 0.694$, $T^2 = 8.746$ and $F = 2.852$ with 3 and 90 d.f. The associated probability value is 0.042.

Display 5.12 Confidence Regions for Differences in Mean Vectors

We can construct a simultaneous confidence interval for $a'(\mu_1 - \mu_2)$, where a is some chosen weight vector of appropriate dimension, using the two sample means $\bar{x}_1$ and $\bar{x}_2$. The $100(1-\alpha)\%$ simultaneous confidence intervals for $a'(\mu_1 - \mu_2)$ are given by

$$a'(\bar{x}_1 - \bar{x}_2) \pm [a'(n_1 S_1 + n_2 S_2)a p(n_1 + n_2)F_{p,m;\alpha}/n_1 n_2 m]^{\frac{1}{2}}$$

where $m = n_1 + n_2 - p - 1$.

For the components of IQ data we can obtain intervals for P, V and Q by taking in turn a' to be [1,0,0], [0,1,0] and [0,0,1], to give the intervals

(a)   P: −0.208 to 14.87
(b)   V: −5.80 to 10.48
(c)   Q: −4.27 to 11.19

FRANCES
Are the problems with outliers the same as when dealing with a single variable?

SIDNEY
Essentially yes, and resistant measures of covariance and correlation are available. Multivariate non-parametric methods, however, are not well developed, partly because of the lack of a natural way to rank order multivariate data. One point about outliers and multivariate data that should be noted is that an observation might now be designated an outlier because of a gross deviation from the body of the data on a single variable, or minor deviations on several variables. Consequently, the detection of outliers may be more of a problem here than with univariate data.

6

Comparing More Than Two Groups on One or More Dimensions: Univariate and Multivariate Analysis of Variance; Analysis of Covariance

6.1 Introduction

The comparison of two groups on some particular variable of interest can be made using the t-test or some non-parametric equivalent, as discussed in the previous chapter. When more than two groups are to be compared, *analysis of variance* procedures are needed. In this chapter, Frances and Sidney discuss the simplest of these procedures and the models that underlie them.

FRANCES
As well as looking at the effect of the mother's postnatal depression on child development, I would also like to examine how the father's psychiatric condition affects the children's IQ and other measures. With this in mind I have categorised the fathers into those who have been treated for psychiatric disorder and those who have not. Combining this with the depression/no depression dichotomy for the mothers I now have four groups to compare rather than two. I assume that I need to use some form of analysis of variance?

6.2 One-way Analysis of Variance—Comparing More Than Two Groups

SIDNEY
That's correct, and if we assume for the present that you simply want to compare the four groups you mentioned with respect to their children's IQ scores, then a simple one-way analysis of variance procedure would be appropriate.

Display 6.1 Multiple Tests—Problems

The problem with computing multiple t-tests when data from several samples are involved is that the type 1 error rate changes. The greater the number of t-tests, the more the type 1 error rate increases beyond the intended α level. This can be quantified as follows.

If c t-tests are performed each at significance level α the overall type 1 error rate becomes

$$1 - (1 - \alpha)^c$$

giving the following values for $\alpha = 0.05$ and particular values of c.

Number of Tests	p
1	0.05
2	0.0975
3	0.142625
4	0.1854938
5	0.2262191
6	0.2649081
10	0.4012631
20	0.6415141

FRANCES

Can you just remind me why it's not suitable to simply perform a t-test and compare each pair of groups?

SIDNEY

The main problem is that doing so increases the probability of rejecting a true hypothesis falsely. Here, there are six t-tests to perform; if each is carried out at the 5% significance level, then even when there are no real differences between the group means, there is a 26% chance of declaring at least one of the comparisons significant (see Display 6.1). The situation gets worse, of course, as the number of groups and therefore the number of comparisons increase.

FRANCES

So I do need to use the analysis of variance approach. As far as I remember this involves a comparison of variances to test a hypothesis about the equality of a set of means, which seems a little curious. Could you explain?

SIDNEY

The null hypothesis here is simply that the four population means are equal. The analysis of variance essentially derives two variances. One is based on variation *between* groups—in other words, variation caused by differences between group means. The other is based on the variation due to differences between the scores *within* each group, that is, differences between individuals within each group that have nothing to do with group differences. This is sometimes known as the *error variance* because

Display 6.2 One-way Analysis of Variance on IQ Scores

(a) All Observations

Source	SS	d.f.	MS	F	p
Groups	5361.30	3	1787.10	7.11	0.0002
Error	22608.02	90	251.20		

(b) Two Outliers Excluded

Source	SS	d.f.	MS	F	p
Groups	1818.43	3	606.14	3.80	0.013
Error	14036.18	88	159.50		

those individual differences may be largely due to uncontrolled variables and imprecise measurement. If the null hypothesis is true, that is, the group means are equal, then both these sample variances estimate the *same* population value. Alternatively, if the group means differ, the one based on between-group variation estimates something *different* and *larger* than the population variance. In that case, group membership is the main reason why individuals differ from each other. Consequently, by assessing the equality or otherwise of the two variances by using an F-test, you are actually also testing whether or not your hypothesis of the equality of group means is reasonable. For your four groups the one-way analysis of variance F-test suggests that the means are not the same, although the presence of the outliers discussed previously may be distorting the comparison, and we should perhaps repeat the analysis with those particular observations removed (see Display 6.2).

FRANCES
Both results seem to indicate that the group means differ, although once the outlier is removed the difference is much less significant. Are the assumptions underlying the significance tests in the analysis of variance much the same as in the two-sample t-test?

SIDNEY
Yes, those of normality and homogeneity. The group distributions should approximate a normal curve and the variability in each group should be comparable to that within each other group. If there is any evidence of a gross departure from either or both assumptions, then some thought should be given to transforming the variable of interest before analysis. As with the t-test, analysis of variance tests are relatively robust against departures from normality although this assumption is more critical in cases where the number of observations in each group differ greatly as they do here. One very quick and simple method of informally looking at the homogeneity assumption is to make a plot of group means against group

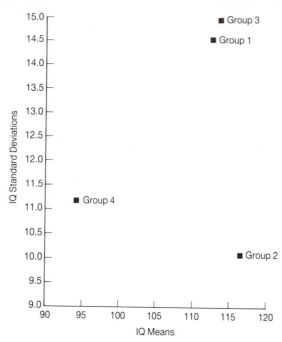

Display 6.3   IQ Means v IQ Standard Deviations

Display 6.4 Model for One-way Analysis of Variance Designs

The following model is assumed for the dependent variable:

$$y_{ij} = \mu + \alpha_i + \epsilon_{ij}$$

where y_{ij} is the j-th observation in the i-th group, μ=grand mean of population, α_i=effect of group i and ϵ_{ij}=experimental error.

---

variances before any analysis. Any evidence of a relationship between the two measures indicates the need for a transformation (see Chapter 2). Such a plot for the IQ data gives little cause for concern (see Display 6.3).

Understanding this simple and other more complex analysis of variance procedures becomes easier if we keep in mind the mathematical *model* upon which the procedures are based. For the one-way analysis of variance the model for the observations is particularly straightforward (see Display 6.4), but it should always be kept in mind that, if you feel that the assumed model does not reflect the psychological or behavioural reality, then you should *not* perform operations and analyses on the data that assume that the model is true.

FRANCES
I now have an overall answer to my question as to whether the four groups differ with respect to IQ scores—yes, they do appear to be different. I

would now like to investigate further to see whether the groups all differ from each other, or whether some have the same average IQ. Is this the situation for *multiple comparison* procedures?

SIDNEY
It may be, but such procedures are not free from criticism and controversy, and many statisticians question the need and appropriateness of *any* multiple comparison approach. But the methods have been around for a long while and many researchers seem to have found them useful. Essentially, all the various multiple comparison procedures that have been suggested try to protect the investigator from obtaining spurious overall and/or specific significant results that can arise from multiple testing, as we saw earlier. One of the simplest procedures consists of performing multiple t-tests, each at level $\alpha^* = \alpha/\text{number of comparisons}$; for example, in our four-group case, the six possible t-tests might each be performed at a level $0.05/6$, which is approximately 1%. This is generally known as the *Bonferroni* procedure.

Another useful and relatively simple procedure, invented by Scheffé, involves the application of multiple t-tests, each judged against a larger critical value than usual. Let's examine what happens when this technique is used on your IQ data (see Display 6.5).

FRANCES
Can we set up confidence intervals in this case where we're dealing with more than two groups?

SIDNEY
Confidence intervals for the difference in means of each pair of groups could be found in the usual way, substituting the critical value based on the F-distribution rather than the t-value.

FRANCES
Well, it looks as though the real impact of the mother's illness on the child's IQ occurs in the groups where the father has had a history of psychiatric illness. For those families, the child's IQ is significantly lower if the mother has also been depressed. Doesn't this seem as though the two factors are working together?

6.3 Two-Way Designs

SIDNEY
Exactly. Although we've carried out a series of analyses on the four groups of data, we have not, as yet, taken any account of the way in which these groups actually arise, in the sense that what you really have is a two-factor design with each factor at two levels.

FRANCES
That's correct of course: husband's psychiatric condition, ill or not, and mother depressed, yes or no. So what I really need to use is a two-way analysis of variance?

Display 6.5 Scheffe's Multiple Comparison Procedure

A procedure for making all possible comparisons between a set of means proposed by Scheffé (1953) involves comparing each t-statistic with the following critical value:

$$\sqrt{(k-1)F_{1-\alpha}(k-1, v)}$$

where k is the number of groups, α is the significance level required and v is the degrees of freedom of the error term from the analysis of variance.

The relevant t-statistics for the maternal depression/husband's psychiatric condition example are as follows:

Comparison	t-statistic
Group 1 v Group 2	−0.48
Group 1 v Group 3	−0.05
Group 1 v Group 4	3.35
Group 2 v Group 3	0.34
Group 2 v Group 4	3.10
Group 3 v Group 4	2.52

How groups are defined:

	Group			
	1	2	3	4
Maternal depression	No	No	Yes	Yes
Husband psychiatric condition	No	Yes	No	Yes

In this case $k = 4$ and $v = 88$ so that the required critical value for $\alpha = 0.05$ is 2.87. Consequently Group 1 and Group 4 are declared to have different means as are Groups 2 and 4.

SIDNEY

I think so. In this case, the appropriate model includes terms not only for psychiatric condition and depression effects but also for the possible *interaction* (see Display 6.6). The corresponding analysis of variance table will contain sums of squares and mean squares corresponding to each of these terms.

FRANCES

How do the results match up with those obtained by analysing the data simply as four groups?

SIDNEY

Well, the three degrees of freedom for the between-groups sum of squares

---

Display 6.6 Two-way Analysis of Variance on IQ Data

The model is now

$$y_{ijk} = \mu + \alpha_i + \beta_j + \gamma_{ij} + \epsilon_{ijk}$$

where y_{ijk} is the k-th observation in level i of the first factor and level j of the second, α_i represents the effect of the i level of the first factor, β_j the effect of the j-th level of the second factor and γ_{ij} the interaction effect.

The results for Frances' data, excluding two outliers, are as follows:

Source	SS	d.f.	MS	F	p
Father	469.55	1	469.55	2.94	0.090
Mother	849.40	1	849.40	5.33	0.023
Interaction	881.57	1	881.57	5.53	0.021
Error	14036.18	88	159.50		

---

from the one-way analysis have been separated into three single degree of freedom sums of squares representing variation between the two levels of father's psychiatric condition, the two levels of maternal depression and the interaction between the two factors. Let's have a look at the results found from analysing the data without the two outliers, since we've agreed previously that these observations should properly be excluded (see Display 6.6).

FRANCES
The analysis seems to indicate that there is an interaction—I think I understand what this means but perhaps you could remind me of the details.

SIDNEY
The interaction represents the possible *non-additivity* of the two main effects. When it is found to be significant it suggests that the difference in IQ scores for the depressed and non-depressed groups amongst those marriages where the father is well is *not* the same as the corresponding difference in IQ scores in marriages where the father has had a psychiatric condition. Some diagrams are useful here to illustrate the various possibilities (see Display 6.7). When a significant interaction is found, it generally becomes of little interest to look at the main effects, since comparisons of levels of a factor *averaged* over the levels of the other factor are unlikely to be very informative.

FRANCES
It seems you could describe this interaction two ways round. You could say that the mother's depression is a risk factor only when the father also has had psychiatric treatment. Alternatively, you could say that the father's illness is important only if the mother gets depressed. Also, what if the two factors are not independent? What if mothers are more likely to get depressed if their husbands have had psychiatric problems in the past?

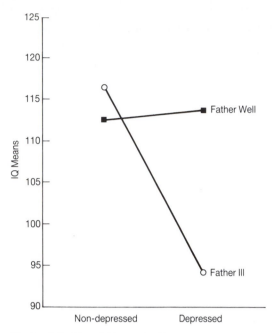

Display 6.7   Plot of Means for IQ Data

SIDNEY

I'm afraid that such questions are very difficult to answer with this type of observational study. It's generally impossible to get at the underlying *causal* mechanisms. You of course haven't randomly assigned these people to become ill or to marry each other or not. There is one further complication that we need to consider, which is caused by the four cells in your 2×2 design having *different* numbers of observations. In such a case, the association of a sum of squares to a particular effect in the model is not so straightforward as in the equal cell sizes case. The problem with the unequal cell sizes design is that the order in which the various sums of squares are calculated becomes important. For example, in the analysis of variance table for your IQ data, the sum of squares for depression should actually be regarded as exploring the effect of mother's depression *controlling* for father's psychiatric condition. In other words, is there a maternal depression effect over and above anything arising solely due to the psychiatric condition and the inequitable distribution of well and ill cases within the two depression groups? We could have performed an analysis reversing the order and testing the effect of psychiatric condition controlling for depression (see Display 6.8).

FRANCES

Is there any statistical reason why I would do it in one order rather than another? Or does that simply depend on how I've set up my question?

Display 6.8 Two-way Analysis of Variance–Different Order of Main Effects

Source	SS	d.f.	MS	F	p
Mother	565.29	1	565.29	3.54	0.063
Father	371.57	1	371.57	2.33	0.131
Interaction	881.57	1	881.57	5.53	0.021

SIDNEY
It largely depends on the question you're trying to answer.

FRANCES
What about testing the interaction effect? Is this still tested first as usual?

SIDNEY
Yes, and if it is found to be significant, testing stops for the reasons we discussed earlier. The same principle applies in more complex multi-factor designs where the most complex interactions are tested first and testing is stopped when a non-zero interaction or main effect is found.

FRANCES
How would I have proceeded if I had considered my data unsuitable for analysis of variance procedures because of non-normality, heterogeneity or both—are there non-parametric equivalents I could have used?

SIDNEY
For the one- and two-way designs we have been considering, there are non-parametric procedures, for example, the *Kruskal–Wallis one-way analysis by ranks*, which do not assume normality. But, it has to be said, these procedures are used relatively rarely. Most statisticians usually prefer model based analysis of variance procedures with the data transformed if necessary to achieve normality and homogeneity.

FRANCES
Well, I now seem to have a relatively clear picture of the effect of depression and father's psychiatric history on the children's IQ scores, but, as yet, I have not considered the separate scales making up the IQ score. How should I proceed if I want to investigate these?

6.4 Multivariate Analysis of Variance

SIDNEY
If you are really interested in the comparison of the set of variables *simultaneously*, then you should apply a *multivariate analysis of variance* procedure analogous to the Hotelling's T^2 test we discussed earlier (see Chapter 5). The approach is again based on the need to find a combination of variables that properly demonstrates any difference between the groups. What we try to do is to identify a derived variable, in general a *weighted sum* of the original variables, on which the groups are well

---

Display 6.9 Multivariate Test Criteria

All four test criteria are based on particular functions of three matrices—these are

T—The matrix of total sums of squares and cross products
W—The matrix of within groups sums of squares and cross products
B—The matrix of between groups sums of squares and cross products

These are analogous to the between, within and total sums of squares in a one-way analysis of variance and satisfy a similar relationship, i.e.

$$\mathbf{T} = \mathbf{W} + \mathbf{B}$$

The three test criteria are as follows:

(a)   *Wilks' Λ*

$$\Lambda = \frac{|\mathbf{W}|}{|\mathbf{T}|}$$

$$= \frac{|\mathbf{W}|}{|\mathbf{B} + \mathbf{W}|}$$

(b)   *Hotelling–Lawley trace*

The sum of the eigenvalues of $\mathbf{BW}^{-1}$

(c)   *The Pillai–Bartlett trace*

The sum of the eigenvalues of $\mathbf{BT}^{-1}$

Each of these statistics can be transformed into approximate F-statistics to enable tests to be undertaken.

---

separated. The derived variables (there may be more than one) are known as *canonical variates* and these form the basis of the multivariate comparison. Unfortunately, in the multivariate situation when there are more than two groups, no single test statistic can be derived that is always the most powerful for detecting *all* types of departure from the null hypothesis which states that the groups being compared have the same mean vector. The three test statistics that have been proposed, the *Pillai–Bartlett trace, Wilks' lambda* and the *Hotelling–Lawley trace* (see Display 6.9) may therefore give different results when used on the same set of data. Let's have a look at what happens when each test statistic is applied to your four groups (ignoring the separate factors for the moment), to compare the three components of IQ (see Display 6.10).

FRANCES
Although I can see the general principle behind the multivariate approach, I am not certain I understand the detail, and perhaps that doesn't matter too much. My intuitive sense of what MANOVA does is this: we could

Display 6.10 Multivariate Analysis of Variance for Components of IQ Data (Excluding Two Outliers)

Test	Value	Approx *F*	d.f.	*p*
Pillai	0.20027	2.10	9, 264.00	0.030
Hotelling	0.22140	2.08	9, 254.00	0.032
Wilks	0.81007	2.10	9, 209.45	0.030

simply combine all the subscales together by adding them up to get a total score. Essentially this means they all receive a weight of one, and are all treated as equally useful bits of information in comparing the groups. But that assumption ignores the fact that the scores correlate with each other, and this has to be taken into consideration when deciding what unique information each scale provides. The MANOVA approach decides how to add them all up to get the best discrimination possible among groups, using weights other than one.

SIDNEY
That's a very reasonable explanation.

FRANCES
But one problem I can see is how to choose the appropriate test criterion, particularly in those cases where the three methods *disagree* on the significance of a comparison.

SIDNEY
That is a very good point, and one where the answer is not clear-cut. As we discussed earlier, one of the most important considerations in selecting a test statistic is the power that it has to detect that the alternative hypothesis is true. Unfortunately, the relative power of the three test statistics we have discussed depends on the way in which the group mean vectors in the underlying populations depart from the null hypothesis of equality. For example, the mean vector might show a consistent trend for each variable, or there might be a departure from equality in all directions. In the first case the Pillai statistic is the *least* powerful and in the second case it is the *most* powerful. So you can see that there is a problem with making a general recommendation.

FRANCES
But if you could only use one of the three test statistics which one would *you* choose? In most articles I read, people seem to use Wilks' lambda.

SIDNEY
Well, if pushed, I would select the Pillai statistic, my reasons being that it is less sensitive to departures from *multivariate normality* and that consistent departures from the null hypothesis, the situation in which this particular criterion is least powerful, are likely to be less common than departures in all directions.

Display 6.11 Multivariate Analysis of Components of IQ Data (Two Outliers Excluded)

(a) Maternal Depression by Husband's Psychiatric History

Test	Value	Approx F	d.f.		p
Pillai	0.05377	1.65	3	87	0.184
Hotelling	0.05683	1.65	3	87	0.184
Wilks	0.94623	1.65	3	87	0.184

(b) Maternal Depression/Husband's Psychiatric History

Test	Value	Approx F	d.f.		p
Pillai	0.07169	2.24	3	87	0.09
Hotelling	0.07723	2.24	3	87	0.09
Wilks	0.92831	2.24	3	87	0.09

(c) Husband's Psychiatric History

Test	Value	Approx F	d.f.		p
Pillai	0.05311	1.63	3	87	0.19
Hotelling	0.05609	1.63	3	87	0.19
Wilks	0.94689	1.63	3	87	0.19

FRANCES
Should we now reanalyse the data using the multivariate approach but taking into account the 2×2 design?

SIDNEY
Yes, we should, and we can find a table analogous to that produced by a univariate analysis of variance (see Display 6.11). Note that in this case, since each comparison involves a single degree of freedom, the results from the three test criteria are equivalent.

FRANCES
Unlike the univariate findings, the MANOVA results imply that there is no interaction effect of the mother's illness and the father's psychiatric history on the child's IQ as indicated by the three component scores. Which result should I believe? Is it possible that these factors affect some components of the IQ and not others? Can I go ahead and look at the univariate ANOVAS on each subscale, even though the multivariate test statistic is not significant?

SIDNEY
Unfortunately, your experience with this example is not untypical when

---

Display 6.12 Univariate Analysis of Variance for Component IQ Scores

Interaction Effects

PP: $F=2.12$, d.f.$=1,88$, $p=0.149$
V: $F=5.25$, d.f.$=1,88$, $p=0.024$
Q: $F=4.02$, d.f.$=1,88$, $p=0.048$

---

using MANOVA procedures and it can be confusing. My view is that it is perfectly reasonable to look at group comparisons of the component IQ scores if these really are of particular interest, even when the MANOVA test is non-significant. In this case we find significant interaction effects for V and Q but not for PP (see Display 6.12).

FRANCES
There is still something that makes the results of these analyses hard to interpret. What if there was something about the child that made the mothers more likely to become depressed, but that had its own direct effects on later IQ? One possibility is damage to the nervous system during the birth process itself. That could create a difficult baby, which might make the mother more likely to become depressed, but it could also affect IQ directly.

6.5 Analysis of Covariance

SIDNEY
Probably what is needed is an analysis of covariance with a score measuring *birth hazards* being used as a covariate. Essentially, the analysis of covariance is a special form of the analysis of variance which allows for variables not explicitly of interest in the investigation, but which might affect the dependent variable in some way. The model for such an analysis is the same as for the equivalent analysis of variance with the addition of a term which allows for a *linear* effect of the covariate on the dependent variable (see Display 6.13).

In the analysis of covariance the variation in the covariate(s) is regarded as a nuisance because it disturbs the values of the variate actually under study. In simple terms, the means of the dependent variable in the various groups are adjusted to correspond to the same mean values of the covariates and then compared by the usual analysis of variance tests. The main assumptions of this type of analysis are firstly linearity and secondly that the linear relationship between the dependent variable and the covariates is the same in each group.

FRANCES
So would the analysis of covariance only really be necessary if the group means differed on one or other of the covariates?

SIDNEY
No. Even when the group means on the covariates are similar, the intro-

---

Display 6.13 Analysis of Covariance Model

$$y_{ij} = \mu + \alpha_i + \beta x_{ij} + \epsilon_{ij}$$

where x_{ij} is the covariate value. In the case of a two factor design with a single covariate as in the IQ example, the model becomes

$$y_{ijk} = \mu + \alpha_i + \gamma_j + \delta_{ij} + \beta_1 x_{ijk} + \epsilon_{ijk}$$

Display 6.14 Analysis of Covariance on IQ Scores (Outliers Excluded)

Source	SS	d.f.	MS	F	p	Regression Coefficients
Father	641.24	1	641.64	3.99	0.05	
Mother/Father	225.21	1	225.21	1.40	0.24	
Interaction	838.55	1	838.55	5.21	0.025	
Birth Hazard	37.54	1	37.54	0.23	0.63	−0.24
Error	13998.6	87	160.90			

duction of the covariate can have the effect of reducing the error variance, resulting of course in more sensitive tests.

FRANCES
So does that mean that an analysis of covariance can still be useful if the groups have been formed by random allocation?

SIDNEY
Certainly, and in fact this was the situation for which the technique was originally designed. Nowadays, of course, it is much more often used to adjust differences between naturally occurring groups in investigations like your own. This is not without its dangers, not least of which is the tendency to encourage researchers to believe that this form of "statistical control" can overcome the problems of investigations in which random allocation is not possible. I think it's about time that we looked at the results of an analysis of covariance on your IQ data (see Display 6.14).

Here the covariate makes very little difference to the results from the original analysis of variance, simply because it is very weakly related to the IQ score. The adjusted IQ means in each group are almost identical to the original values (see Display 6.15).

FRANCES
Both the analysis of variance and analysis of covariance models look similar to regression equations—are they?

SIDNEY
Essentially they are identical, which explains why they are all subsumed

Display 6.15 IQ Means—Raw and Adjusted for Birth Hazards (Outliers Excluded)

| | | Father Psychiatric Problem | | | |
| | | No | | Yes | |
		Raw	Adjusted	Raw	Adjusted
Mother depressed	No	112.62	112.56	116.50	116.61
	Yes	113.67	113.55	82.17	94.60

Display 6.16 General Multiple Regression Model

If the response variable is denoted as y and the *explanatory* or *independent* variables as $x_1, x_2, \ldots, x_p$, the general multiple regression model can be written as

$$y_i = \beta_0 + \beta_1 x_{1i} + \beta_2 x_{2i} + \cdots + \beta_p x_{pi} + \epsilon_i$$

The coefficients $\beta_1, \ldots, \beta_p$ represent the effect of the corresponding explanatory variable on the response variable *given* that the remaining explanatory variables are constant, in the sense that a change of one unit in explanatory variable, x_j, produces a change of β_j units in y.

under what is usually known as the *generalised linear model*. Recall that, in the simplest case, a regression equation states that a response value is a function of a single explanatory variable plus measurement error, $y = \beta x + \varepsilon$ (see Chapter 2). In the analysis of variance, of course, the variables are generally categorical, dummy variables representing different levels of a factor. In regression examples these variables are more commonly continuous. The analysis of covariance model contains both continuous and categorical variables on the right-hand side of the equation. It is easy to write down a general form for the model which could cover many situations (see Display 6.16).

7

The Analysis of Repeated Measures Designs

7.1 Introduction

One of the most common research paradigms is that where subjects are observed at several different time points and the values of some variables of interest recorded at each. Each subject may, for example, be observed at two time points, perhaps before and after treatment. Although the same construct is measured at each time point, the problem is often regarded as involving *two* dependent variables rather than *one* insofar as two distinct measurements are involved. Note that this differs from the traditional way in which psychologists depicted repeated measures designs, where the two measurements were presented as two levels of another, "within subjects" independent variable. In general, when more than two time points are of concern, an investigation in which *repeated* measures are made on subjects can be regarded as *multivariate*. In such investigations, it is unlikely to be simple between-group differences at each individual time point that are of most interest, but rather differences in the way the groups proceed over time. Such questions involve *combinations* of the responses at each of the time points, that is, combinations of the repeated measures, usually in specifically structured ways.

In this chapter, Frances and Sidney discuss repeated measures designs, paying particular attention to whether univariate or multivariate tests should be used and the assumptions made by each.

FRANCES
One of the main components of my study was *longitudinal*, the fortnightly ratings made of mothers' dysphoria. I would now like to investigate how

these ratings develop and change over the 24 weeks of the study. In particular, of course, I would like to see if the time progression is different for the various treatment groups. Is a repeated measures analysis of variance the appropriate procedure?

7.2   Repeated Measures Analysis of Variance

SIDNEY
Yes, I think you are probably right. But such analyses are not always simple or straightforward and there are a number of possible approaches. The one adopted by many researchers is to deal with repeated measures designs using conventional univariate analysis of variance techniques. In your study, for example, the repeated measures would basically be treated as if each measurement arose from a different individual, in other words, as if the observations were independent without the complication of being repeated. The variation in the data is then partitioned into a part due to differences *between subjects* and a part due to differences *within subjects*, with the latter being further divided into components representing variation between time points and variation due to the groups × time interaction. The model underlying such an analysis assumes that subjects are randomly selected from some population of interest and consequently that differences between them are represented by a *random* effect. The time points involved are, however, considered to be of specific interest, and so change within individuals over time is represented in the model by a *fixed* effects parameter. This leads to what is usually referred to as a *mixed model*.

If for the moment we consider only the mothers who had all twelve dysphoria scores recorded, then this simple analysis of your data leads to the following results (see Display 7.1). How might you interpret the results of the F-tests?

FRANCES
Well, at first sight it looks disappointing; it looks as though the prevention programme has failed to work. There is no main effect of either the child development training programme or the family therapy. But what does seem interesting is the interactions with the time variable. It looks as though the women in the two different treatment groups are responding differently as the weeks go on.

SIDNEY
It is often helpful to supplement formal analyses of this kind by drawing a graph; in this case, plotting the repeated measures mean profiles for each treatment group may be informative (see Display 7.2). Can you make any sense out of the graph?

FRANCES
Yes, I think so. It looks as though the women who are doing best at the end of the six months are those who had experienced the child development training alone; the family therapy treatment only seems to cause the dysphoria scores to get progressively worse. The combined effect of both

Display 7.1 Repeated Measures Analysis of Dysphoria Scores

Analysis of Variance Table

Between Subjects

Source	S-of-Sq.	d.f.	Mean Sq.	F	P
Child Dev.(T1)	54.38	1	54.38	2.48	0.12
Family Therap.(T2)	37.64	1	37.64	1.72	0.20
T1 × T2	18.89	1	18.89	0.86	0.36

Within Subjects

Source	S-of-Sq.	d.f.	Mean Sq.	F	P
Time	24.97	11	2.27	1.34	0.20
Time × T1	74.86	11	6.80	4.01	0.00
Time × T2	86.78	11	7.89	4.65	0.00
T × T1 × T2	13.37	11	1.21	0.72	0.72
Error	690.60	407	1.70		

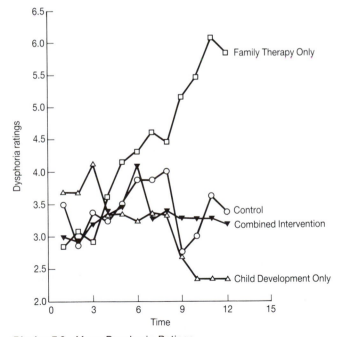

Display 7.2 Mean Dysphoria Ratings

Display 7.3 Compound Symmetry

A covariance matrix displaying compound symmetry has the following form

$$\mathbf{S} = \begin{pmatrix} \sigma^2 & & & \\ \rho\sigma^2 & \sigma^2 & & \\ \rho\sigma^2 & \rho\sigma^2 & \sigma^2 & \\ \vdots & \vdots & & \\ \rho\sigma^2 & \rho\sigma^2 & \cdots & \sigma^2 \end{pmatrix}$$

(Elements on the main diagonal represent variances; off-diagonal elements represent covariances between pairs of variables.)

Note that *all* diagonal elements are equal and *all* off-diagonal elements are equal.

---

treatments keeps the scores at about the same level as the control group. These results certainly seem straightforward—so where do the complications arise?

SIDNEY

Well, let's begin with the assumptions behind this approach. As always, normality of the response variable is assumed but this creates no new problems. More critical is the assumption of the *compound symmetry* of the repeated measures.

FRANCES

What exactly is compound symmetry?

SIDNEY

This involves the variances and covariances of the repeated measures. Compound symmetry implies that the responses corresponding to different levels of the repeated factor must have equal variances and that their pairwise covariances are also equal. So the *covariance matrix* of the repeated measures should have a very special form (see Display 7.3 and Chapter 5). When more than a single group is involved a further assumption is that of the equality of this covariance matrix across groups.

FRANCES

In other words, you're saying that the total amount of variability of each dysphoria measure should be about the same at each time point, and the relationship between scores at time 1 and time 2 say should be about equivalent to the relationship between scores at, for example, time 5 and time 7. Does that mean that the relationship between scores at any two points in time must be equal to the relationship at any other two points? Isn't this a lot to ask? Should we test this assumption before carrying out the usual analysis of variance or can we simply assume it will hold in most situations?

SIDNEY

There are tests of compound symmetry and equality of covariance matrices that can be applied, but in general they are not used simply because the compound symmetry assumption is most *unlikely* to be realistic in most investigations. It is indeed a lot to ask of your data. Let me explain. Suppose the repeated measures factor involves time, as it does in your example; then compound symmetry implies that two measurements separated by a large time interval have the same covariance as two measurements separated by a small time interval. Intuitively, however, it seems more likely that the latter pair of measurements will be more strongly related than the former.

FRANCES
In the case of postnatal dysphoria, there are also reasons why you might expect the variance at each testing point to decrease systematically over time. For example, what if every mother gets more dysphoric over time, regardless of treatment condition? Alternatively, what if everyone gets a bit happier when their babies start sleeping through the night? That should also affect the relationship between testing points that are close vs. distant in time.

SIDNEY
That's right, and it leads to problems. If compound symmetry does not hold then the actual significance level of the univariate F-tests will *exceed* the significance level set at the beginning of the study—too many true null hypotheses will be rejected.

FRANCES
So what can we do? Should we set a more conservative significance level at the outset?

SIDNEY
There are a number of possibilities. One would be to summarise each individual's profile of repeated measures in terms of a single statistic, such as a regression coefficient or perhaps the area under the curve. I'll say more about this approach later.

Perhaps the most common way to deal with departures from compound symmetry is to introduce a *correction factor* into the degrees of freedom of the univariate F-tests. This correction factor reflects the degree of departure from compound symmetry, taking the value 1 if the assumption holds and values less than 1 where it does not. The correction factor may be estimated from the data in two ways, although in most cases both methods give very similar results. Let's look at the calculations involved and how the correction factor is used (see Display 7.4).

Using this approach on your data leads to new F-tests for time and the interactions of time with treatments (see Display 7.5); although here the conclusions are largely the same as when using the unadjusted tests, the probability value for the time × family therapy interaction does change.

FRANCES
All the results appear to indicate that there are differences between the treatment groups with respect to how the dysphoria scores develop over time. How should I go about investigating these differences in a little more detail?

Display 7.4 Correction Factors for Repeated Measure Designs

(a) *Greenhouse and Geisser (1959)*

$$\epsilon_1 = p^2(\bar{\sigma}_{tt} - \bar{\sigma}_{..}^2/(p-1)(\sum\sum\sigma_{ts}^2 - 2p\sum\bar{\sigma}_{t.}^2 + p^2\bar{\sigma}_{..}^2)$$

where p is the number of repeated measures on each subject, $\sigma_{ts}, t = 1, \ldots, p, s = 1, \ldots, p$ represent the elements of the *population* covariance matrix of the repeated measures, and the remaining terms are various sums and sums of squares of these elements.

(b) *Huynh and Feldt (1990)*

$$\epsilon = \min(1, a/b)$$

where $a = n(p-1)\epsilon_1 - 2$ and $b = (p-1)[n - g - (p-1)\epsilon_1]$ with n being the number of subjects and g the number of groups.

The correction factor has a maximum value of 1.0 achieved when compound symmetry holds; in cases where compound symmetry cannot be assumed the degrees of freedom of F-tests involving occasions are multiplied by the correction factor and consequently *decreased*. Tests comparing groups remain unaltered.

Since the correction factor has to be estimated from the data, a complication is introduced—how will the inaccuracy in the estimate of ϵ influence the results? Greenhouse and Geisser (1959) avoid this problem by suggesting replacing ϵ with its *smallest* possible value, namely $1/(p-1)$. This approach is likely however to be *very* conservative.

7.3   Contrasts between the Repeated Measures

SIDNEY

A useful strategy for a broad range of repeated measurement studies is to view the subjects as the units of analysis in the following two-stage procedure; firstly, particular measures of interest are constructed from the repeated observations within each subject—examples might be sums for total response, differences between particular time points or more complex *contrasts* between the measures. Next, these new variables are analysed either by a series of separate, univariate methods or by simultaneous multivariate methods. The ideas behind this approach are more simply explained by first considering a repeated measures design with just two observations for each subject, so let's begin by considering just the first and the last time point in your example. It will also help if, for the moment, we consider only the child development treatment (T1).

Since we are interested primarily in the change in the dysphoria ratings between the two time points, an analysis based on the *difference* scores of the individuals might be sensible. Suppose then we first take the pair of scores of each individual and calculate the corresponding difference score. A test for a between-groups effect on this derived variable may be made using a one-way analysis of variance (or equivalently here, since

---

Display 7.5 Repeated Measures Analysis of Dysphoria Scores (with Correction Factors)

Analysis of Variance

Within Subjects

Source	G G *(p)*	H F *(p)*
Time	0.264	0.259
Time × T1	0.007	0.004
Time × T2	0.003	0.002
Time × T1 × T2	0.555	0.579

Epsilon factors for degrees of freedom adjustment.

(1)   Greenhouse and Geisser : 0.30

(2)   Huynh and Feldt : 0.35

(GG (p) : Greenhouse and Geisser Prob., *HF (p)* : Huynh and Feldt Prob.)

---

only two groups are involved, an independent means t-test). The question addressed by such a procedure is "Is the average change in dysphoria scores from week 1 to week 24 the same in both treatment groups or is there some difference?" This is, of course, equivalent to asking if there is an *interaction* between treatment group and time. If we find no difference between groups on the change variable or, in other words, no group × time interaction, then we might proceed to investigate whether the average of the time change variable taken over both groups is zero. This is equivalent to asking whether there is a change over time. The appropriate test would arise from the one-way analysis of variance performed on the change variable as the test for the grand mean or constant, a test which in most analyses of variance is of no interest.

FRANCES
So, in such a test, we're asking whether the pattern of change shown in each group differs from the overall pattern of change over time shown by the sample as a whole. The graph certainly indicated that this was the case. But what seems to be missing so far is any equivalent of a test for the simple group difference.

SIDNEY
That's right. So far, use of the derived time-change variable has led to tests for the groups × time interaction and the main effect of time. If no interaction is present, then it would be appropriate to ask about the overall group difference; using the derived variable approach, we would simply calculate the average (or sum) of each mother's first and twenty-

Display 7.6 Transforming the Repeated Measures—A Simple Example Involving Only Two Time Points

(a) *One-way Analysis of Variance of "Sum" Score*

Source	S-of-Sq.	d.f.	Mean Sq.	F	P
Mean	2058.00	1	2058.00	289.86	0.00
Treatment	42.00	1	42.00	5.92	0.02
Error	284.00	40	7.10		

(N.B.: Here the "Mean" line is of no interest—it simply tests whether the grand mean of the dysphoria scores is different from zero.)

The "treatment" line gives a test of difference in level of the two treatment groups.

(b) *One-way Analysis of Variance of "Difference" Score*

Source	S-of-Sq.	d.f.	Mean Sq.	F	P
Mean	16.09	1	16.09	2.23	0.14
Treatment	59.52	1	59.52	8.26	0.01
Error	288.38	40	7.21		

Here the "Mean" line gives a test for the difference between the two occasions and the "treatment" line a test of the occasions × treatment interaction.

Table of Means

	Time 1	Time 12
No Child Development	3.09	4.90
Child Development	3.28	2.71

fourth week's dysphoria ratings. A one-way analysis of variance is then the appropriate test.

So, to summarise—the original two dysphoria ratings for each mother are transformed into a sum and difference score. These two new variables *directly* address the questions of most interest. Before we move on to consider more complicated situations, let's just examine the results from applying the procedure to your data (see Display 7.6).

FRANCES
This approach seems very straightforward. It suggests that there's no overall significant difference in dysphoria between the first and last week of interviewing, but that those women who do and do not experience consultation with the child development specialist differ in that regard. How is the approach extended to designs involving more than two repeated measures?

Display 7.7 Transforming Repeated Measures Coefficients Defining Linear and Quadratic Trends for Designs with Three Time Points

	Time 1	Time 2	Time 3
Linear	-1	0	1
Quadratic	1	-2	1

SIDNEY

The principle is just the same, but the transformations needed to generate new variables that are appropriate to answer specific questions of interest may be more complicated. In examples involving time, a very useful approach is to consider transformations that describe a particular type of change over time. The simplest, for example, would measure the *linear trend* of the response variable, in other words, the rate at which the response changes with time; also of interest might be the *quadratic trend* which gives information about how the rate of change in the response variable *varies* with time. For three equally spaced time points the appropriate transformations of the original variables to give the linear and quadratic trend variables are very simple (see Display 7.7).

FRANCES

I see—the linear trend indicates whether these women are getting either more or less unhappy over time. The quadratic trend might show whether there is an upsurge or decrease in dysphoria in the middle time period. For example, most babies start smiling a lot around three months of age—that might make everyone feel better for a while. But what about my actual data? Can we look at these trends over time more precisely?

SIDNEY

For twelve time points, as in your example, things are a little more complicated (see Display 7.8), but since they will be generated automatically in the statistical software used for analysing repeated measures designs, the additional complexity need not be of any concern. So, if we do find the linear and quadratic trends for all the mothers and use each in a 2×2 analysis of variance involving both treatments, we may be able to say quite a lot about how mothers in the various groups change over time (see Display 7.9—the complication of unequal cell sizes is ignored in this analysis). For example, the analysis of variance of the linear trend variable indicates a significant treatment $\times$ time effect for both the child development treatment and for family therapy. Again some graphs may be helpful in interpreting these results (see Displays 7.10 and 7.11).

FRANCES

Well, it certainly looks as though the two different prevention programmes produce almost opposite linear trends. People who don't receive the child development treatment become progressively more dysphoric over time, as opposed to those who do receive training in child development. On the other hand, there seems to be an iatrogenic effect of our other treatment—

Display 7.8 Transforming Repeated Measures Coefficients Defining Linear and Quadratic Trends for Designs with Twelve Time Points

	T1	T2	T3	T4	T5	T6	T7	T8	T9	T10	T11	T12
Linear	−11	−9	−7	−5	−3	−1	1	3	5	7	9	11
Quadratic	−35	−29	−17	1	25	55	55	25	1	−17	−29	−35

Display 7.9 Analysis of Linear and Quadratic Time Trends for Dysphoria Data

(a) *One-way Analysis of Variance of Linear Trend Variable*

Source	S-of-Sq.	d.f.	Mean Sq.	F	P
Mean	6306.54	1	6306.54	1.23	0.27
Treatment 1	39559.99	1	39559.99	7.73	0.01
Treatment 2	42899.34	1	42899.34	8.38	0.01
T1 × T2	3621.07	1	3621.07	0.71	0.40
Error	189388.81	37	5118.62		

(b) *One-way Analysis of Variance of Quadratic Trend Variable*

Source	S-of-Sq.	d.f.	Mean Sq.	F	P
Mean	100351.43	1	100351.43	2.86	0.10
Treatment 1	2448.87	1	2448.87	0.07	0.79
Treatment 2	4470.93	1	4470.93	0.13	0.72
T1 × T2	33667.67	1	33667.67	0.96	0.33
Error	1297624.45	37	35070.93		

In these two tables the "mean" line gives a test for the trend component, the two treatment lines tests for treatment and trend interaction and the T1 × T2 interaction line, a test for T1 × T2 × trend interaction.

---

people who receive the family therapy programme become progressively more dysphoric as the weeks go on, as opposed to people who are not in family therapy. That's a fairly disturbing finding. One other thing, though; in my study, I have 12 time points so, in theory at least, I could have studied trends more complex than just linear and quadratic—wouldn't this have been useful?

SIDNEY

Unless you have very specific *a priori* hypotheses about particular trend components, I think that, in most cases, looking at the linear and quadratic is sufficient. Perhaps occasionally the cubic trend, which indicates whether the change over time follows an S-shaped curve, is also of interest. More

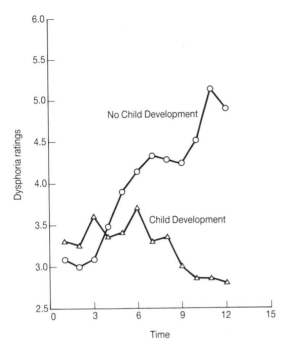

Display 7.10   Mean Dysphoria Ratings

complex terms will, for most investigators, prove extremely difficult to interpret.   One thing to mention if you are looking at a number of trend components is that the tests should be performed in sequence—for example, the cubic component would be examined first; if a significant effect is found, lower-order trends are not examined, since any description of change over time must involve cubic *and* lower-order terms.   If the cubic term is non-significant, then it can be dropped and examination of the quadratic trend takes place.

FRANCES
Originally you mentioned that repeated measures data should be viewed as multivariate rather than univariate, but as far as I can tell you have, as yet, not carried out any multivariate tests. Why?

SIDNEY
It's really a matter of deciding which questions are of most interest here. It would be possible to make a test of the overall hypothesis "Are all the trend components zero?" by using one of the multivariate test criteria discussed previously. However, when dealing with questions about a set of increasingly complex transformed variables such as the set of trend variables we have used, it is unlikely that the primary interest will be simply whether any of them exist. Rather, the important issue is how parsimonious a description of the data can be provided, and this is best addressed by a sequence of univariate *F*-tests for each trend in turn. So

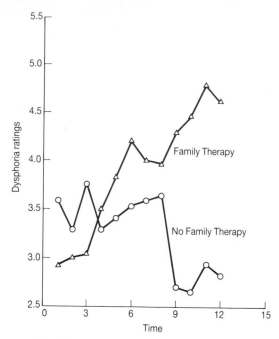

Display 7.11 Mean Dysphoria Ratings

rather than needing to perform a fully multivariate test, we need to apply a *multiple* univariate sequence of tests.

FRANCES

Is it useful, however, to report the multivariate test statistic before going on to explore the univariate findings and contrasts? I see this more and more in the literature. When, for example, would you *not* go on to do the univariate tests?

SIDNEY

The question of the most appropriate procedure to use for repeated measures designs is still a topic much discussed by statisticians and there appears to be no clear consensus. In many situations, however, there will be little to choose between a multivariate test and the modified F-tests and the latter are certainly simpler to interpret. In general, I much prefer the transformed variable approach since it directly addresses those questions of specific interest.

FRANCES

One thing that does cause me concern about the analyses performed on the dysphoria ratings is that we have left out all the mothers who have any of the fortnightly ratings missing. Now I can see that this is unavoidable for mothers who had a considerable number of their ratings missing, but there are some where only a single recording has been missed. Is there no way these could be included?

Display 7.12 Data on Dysphoria Scores for Mothers with at most Three Missing Observations

Obsv.	t1	t2	t3	t4	t5	t6	t7	t8	t9	t10	t11	t12
1	7	7	8	8	7	6	7	8	7	7	3	−9
2	4	4	4	3	7	2	2	2	2	2	−9	−9
3	4	6	6	9	8	8	8	8	8	8	−9	−9
4	3	6	6	6	2	5	3	3	4	4	−9	−9
5	7	8	8	8	9	4	4	3	3	2	−9	−9
6	5	5	5	3	3	3	3	3	3	−9	3	−9
7	2	2	2	2	2	1	1	1	1	−9	−9	−9
8	4	4	4	4	5	5	6	8	6	5	−9	−9
9	3	2	2	2	2	6	6	2	6	6	−9	1

Note that −9 indicates a missing value. The estimation of the missing values involves the 41 complete observations given in Appendix A and the 9 incomplete observations above. For the exercise of estimating the missing observations the data are regarded simply as a set of 50 observations—no account is taken of treatment group.

SIDNEY
There are several approaches to deal with missing observations in general and for repeated measures designs in particular. The most common method is to replace the missing values in some way with suitable estimates. These can range from simple means to values derived from complicated regression type procedures. Such procedures may be useful when the data contain only a small number of missing values, but should not be used when there is a moderate or large amount of missing data. Let's see what happens when we use a very simple replacement method involving means, and a more complex procedure involving regression and an assumption of multivariate normality, on those mothers who have at most three dysphoria values missing (see Display 7.12). Rather different values can result (see Display 7.13), but the more complicated procedure is usually to be preferred.

For repeated measures designs, specialised techniques are available for dealing with missing observations. Essentially, these methods make some assumption about the covariance structure of the repeated measures and estimate the model parameters using the available data. Tests for the usual hypotheses of interest can then be made. These procedures are generally only suitable for designs where the number of repeated measures is relatively small, and would not be able to be applied to your data.

A final point to remember about missing data is that the reason why scores are missing has to be considered, since most replacement methods are only applicable if the data are missing at random. If this is unlikely to be true, then cases with missing observations will have to be dropped entirely.

Display 7.13 Estimated Missing Values for Dysphoria Scores

(a) *Replacement by Means*

Obsv.	t10	t11	t12
1			3.88
2		3.98	3.88
3		3.98	3.88
4		3.98	3.88
5		3.98	3.88
6		3.87	3.88
7	3.87	3.98	3.88
8		3.98	3.88
9		3.98	

(b) *Missing Values estimated by EM algorithm—see Little and Rubin (1987)*

Obsv.	t10	t11	t12
1			2.90
2		3.11	2.68
3		7.05	6.55
4		2.40	3.23
5		1.46	1.24
6	2.82		3.27
7	1.24	1.83	1.70
8		5.55	5.10
9		4.98	

FRANCES

But what if there is selective attrition? What if people tend to drop out more in one treatment group than another? For example, our analyses made it seem as though it was worse to be receiving the family therapy treatment than to be in the control group. But notice that only eight of the original control group members remain in the final sample. Maybe the really dysphoric women in that group simply dropped out of the study altogether. Shouldn't we take a look at this?

SIDNEY

Are you suggesting that the drop-out rate itself is a variable of interest? I think we'd better spend some time in our next meeting looking at that question.

8

Comparing Groups with Respect to Categorical Outcome Measures: Logistic Regression and Survival Analysis

8.1 Introduction

In many situations, particularly in the social and behavioural sciences, the response variables of interest are often *categorical*. In other words, the outcome of interest is not a dimension such as children's IQ scores, as discussed in the preceding chapters. Rather, the outcome is measured in terms of a *dichotomy*, such as "yes" vs "no", "on" vs "off", "ill" vs "well" and so on. Frances's study is designed to prevent the occurrence of postnatal depression and so her primary interest is whether the women in each group fall into one or other of two outcome categories, "well" or "depressed". In this chapter, therefore, Frances and Sidney discuss procedures for analysing such categorical response variables.

FRANCES
The first phase of the prevention study is now completed and the most important thing I have to consider is whether or not the treatment programme did in fact succeed in keeping women from becoming depressed. I initially specified that if any of the dysphoria ratings rose above a value of 6 at any time during the six months assessment period, the woman would be screened by a psychiatrist for depression. We would then be able to determine how many cases of depression occurred in each treatment group. Thus each woman in the study would get a "caseness" score—either she was or was not a case of depression. So I have here the caseness scores for all the women in the sample along with their status with respect to the two treatments—child development training and family therapy. Here I've considered *all* the mothers, even those who had some dysphoria scores missing.

Display 8.1 Chi-square Test on Four Treatment Groups

	Group 1	Group 2	Group 3	Group 4
Depressed	10	8	3	5
Not depressed	5	7	12	10

Group 1 = No Treatment
Group 2 = Family Therapy Only
Group 3 = Child Development Only
Group 4 = Both Treatments.

The chi-square test statistic takes the value 7.87 with 3 d.f. and $p=0.049$. .

Now obviously what I want to do is to determine whether the treatments have any effect on the chance that women become depressed. Since the outcome is categorical—depressed or not—I have simply counted the number of depressed and non-depressed women in all four treatment groups and applied a chi-square test to compare them (see Display 8.1).

SIDNEY
Since the chi-square test is significant, there does seem to be some difference between the four groups with respect to the chance of becoming depressed.

FRANCES
Yes, but what I don't seem to be able to get at is the effects of the separate treatments or their interaction. In addition, I would like to be able to look at the effect of marital conflict on becoming depressed but again I'm not at all sure about the appropriate analysis. What I seem to need is the equivalent of the analysis of variance and covariance techniques we considered earlier (see Chapter 6) but suitable for a categorical response variable. Does such a technique exist?

8.2   Logistic Regression

SIDNEY
Several approaches might be considered. One would be to simply ignore the particular nature of the response variable and apply the usual analysis of variance or covariance procedures in the normal way (see Display 8.2). But since we know in this case that the data are certainly *not* normally distributed, such an analysis is very unappealing; *a priori*, we know that assumptions are not met.

An alternative would be to use an analysis of variance procedure, applied to the *proportion* of women who become depressed. Basically the model is the same as we discussed earlier for the IQ data, except

Display 8.2 Analysis of Variance and Covariance for Depression Data

If we define a response variable taking the value 1 if a woman becomes depressed and 2 if she remains non-depressed and apply the usual ANOVA and ANOCOVA procedures the results are as follows:

(a) *Analysis of Variance*

Source	SS	d.f.	MS	F	p
CD	1.67	1	1.67	7.29	0.0091
FT	0.00	1	0.00	0.00	1.00
CD × FT	0.267	1	0.267	1.17	0.284
Error	12.80	56	0.228		

(b) *Analysis of Covariance*

Source	SS	d.f.	MS	F	p	reg. coeff.
CD	1.335	1	1.335	5.93	0.018	
FT	0.003	1	0.003	0.01	0.912	
CD × FT	0.121	1	0.121	0.54	0.467	
Conflict	0.404	1	0.404	1.79	0.19	0.041
Error	12.396	55	0.225			

that now the response variable is a proportion (see Display 8.3). There is a problem in using this simple-minded approach, which arises because the response variable here is constrained to lie between zero and one. Unfortunately, this constraint is not built into the analysis of variance model, which means that the model could lead to predicted values for the proportions that do not satisfy the constraint. Again, it seems rather unsatisfactory to assume a model that you know *a priori* to be unsuitable for the type of response variable in which you are interested. Fortunately, there is a rather neat way of overcoming the problem and that is simply to transform your proportions in such a way that, instead of ranging from 0 to 1, the transformed value ranges from minus infinity to plus infinity. The transformed variable can then be dealt with in a way that is completely analogous to the usual linear regression models we discussed previously.

FRANCES
So what's the appropriate transformation?

SIDNEY
It's known as the *logistic transformation* and the method of analysis is usually known as *logistic regression* (see Display 8.4). Basically, the transformation involves the natural log of the proportion divided by 1 minus the proportion.

Display 8.3 Analysis of Variance Model for Proportion of Women Becoming Depressed

Observed Proportions for The Two treatments

		Child Development	
		No	Yes
Family Therapy	No	0.67	0.20
	Yes	0.53	0.33

Model for Proportions

$$p_{ij} = \mu + \alpha_i + \beta_j + \epsilon_{ij}$$

Analysis of Variance for Proportions

Source	SS	D.f.	MS	F	p
CD	0.112	1	0.112	6.16	0.244
FT	0.000	1	0.000	0.00	0.976
Error	0.018	1	0.018		

Display 8.4 The Logistic Transformation of a Proportion

The transformation is given by

$$\lambda = \ln \frac{p}{1-p}$$

as p varies from 0 to 1 λ varies from $-\infty$ to $+\infty$.
The inverse of this transformation is

$$p = \frac{\exp(\lambda)}{1 + \exp(\lambda)}$$

FRANCES
So now we simply apply analysis of variance procedures to the logistic transformed proportions?

SIDNEY
Not quite. You have to remember that the response variable here will not have a normal distribution so that, although the basic models look essentially the same as those for continuous variables, the process of fitting the model and estimating its parameters will be rather different. In fact, it involves a process known as *maximum likelihood* but the important thing from your point of view is not the details but the interpretation

Display 8.5 Logistic Regression Applied to Depression Data

The model fitted is

$$\lambda = \beta_0 + \beta_1 x_1 + \beta_2 x_2$$

where λ is the logistic function and x_1 and x_2 are *dummy* variables for the two treatments, with each taking the value 0 when the treatment is not given and 1 when it is given.

The parameter estimates and their standard errors are as follows:

$$\hat{\beta}_0 = 0.4055(0.4640), \quad \hat{\beta}_1 = -1.417(0.5561), \quad \hat{\beta}_2 = 0.0000(0.5532)$$

To assess the possible interaction effect of the two treatments the appropriate model would be

$$\lambda = \beta_0 + \beta_1 x_1 + \beta_2 x_2 + \beta_3 x_1 x_2$$

but it is clear that no interaction effect need be postulated since the chi-square goodness-of-fit statistic for the no-interaction model takes the value 1.24 with 1 d.f.—this model fits very well. The important question now however is "does a simpler model fit equally well?" This question can be addressed by examining the change in the goodness-of-fit measure as each term is added to the model. For these data this gives the following:

Term	Chi-square	D.f.	Change in Chi-square	Change in d.f.
Gr. Mean	8.18	3		
+CD	1.24	2	6.93	1
+FT	1.24	1	0.00	1

Clearly the only significant effect is that produced by the child development treatment.

---

of the parameters and goodness-of-fit measures that result. So let's have a look at what happens when we apply logistic regression to your data on those mothers who become depressed and those who don't, beginning with a model that includes main effect parameters for each of the two treatments (see Display 8.5). Clearly family therapy has no effect in reducing the number of mothers who become depressed from the no treatment situation. On the other hand, learning about child development does appear to reduce the chance of becoming depressed. Let's look in detail at the terms in a logistic model for depression including only a main effect for the child development treatment (see Display 8.6).

FRANCES
Would it be possible to include variables other than those representing treatment effects in such an analysis? Here, as I've mentioned, I'd like to include a measure of marital conflict as a covariate. It looks as if marital

Display 8.6 Logistic Model for Depression Data with Only Child Development Included

The model is now

$$\lambda = \beta_0 + \beta_1 x_1$$

The parameter estimates are $\widehat{\beta}_0 = 0.405(0.3726)$ and $\widehat{\beta}_1 = -1.417(0.5561)$. The predicted values for the probability of becoming depressed are

$$\widehat{p}_{11} = \frac{\exp(\widehat{\beta}_0)}{1 + \exp(\widehat{\beta}_0)}$$

$$\widehat{p}_{21} = \frac{\exp(\widehat{\beta}_0 + \widehat{\beta}_1)}{1 + \exp(\widehat{\beta}_0 + \widehat{\beta}_1)}$$

$$\widehat{p}_{12} = \widehat{p}_{11}$$

$$\widehat{p}_{22} = \widehat{p}_{21}$$

where

p_{11}=Pr(depression given no treatment)
p_{12}=Pr(depression given only family therapy)
p_{21}=Pr(depression given only child development)
p_{22}=Pr(depression given both treatments)

This leads to $\widehat{p}_{11} = 0.600$ and $\widehat{p}_{21} = 0.266$. The corresponding figures for predicted number of women becoming depressed in each treatment group are found by multiplying these estimates by 15 to give

no treatment:	9.0,
child development only:	4.0,
family therapy only:	9.0,
both treatments:	4.0.

conflict is greater in some treatment groups than others. But marital conflict is a continuous variable.

SIDNEY
That presents no problem since the model can quite easily accommodate both categorical and continuous explanatory variables (see Display 8.7). The results indicate that marital conflict has little effect on whether or not a woman becomes depressed.

FRANCES
Could you say a little more about how to interpret these coefficients?

SIDNEY
The interpretation of the regression coefficients is essentially the same as in the usual multiple regression situation, although it has to be remembered that we are now dealing with the transformed response. So, for example, being given the child development treatment decreases the logistic trans-

Display 8.7 Logistic Model for Depression—Child Development, Family Therapy and Marital Conflict

Term	Coeff.	SE	Coeff/SE	Exp(coeff)	95%CI Lower	Upper
CD	−1.32	0.57	−2.33	0.27	0.08	0.83
FT	0.08	0.57	0.16	1.09	0.35	3.41
Conflict	0.21	0.14	1.56	1.24	0.94	1.63

Comparing each coefficient divided by its standard error, with the 5% normal deviate, 1.96, shows that only the coefficient for child development is significantly different from zero.

formed response by 1.32 compared to not receiving this treatment. A more appealing interpretation is available if we consider the transformed response in a little more detail. The term $p/(1 - p)$ gives the *odds* of being depressed to not being depressed; if the ratio is greater than 1, then the odds are in favour of depression. Consequently, the logistic transformation is simply ln(odds). So, by exponentiating a coefficient, we obtain the effect of the corresponding variable on the odds. For example, for the child development treatment, we obtain the value 0.27 with 95% confidence interval (0.08 to 0.83). This implies that the odds of becoming depressed amongst mothers receiving the child development treatment is about a quarter of that for mothers not receiving this treatment.

For marital conflict the exponentiated regression coefficient is 1.24. So, a unit increase in marital conflict multiplies the odds of becoming depressed rather than remaining non-depressed by 24%, although of course the effect is not significantly different from zero.

FRANCES
The conclusion reached from the logistic regression analysis appears to be exactly what we would have reached using the results of the inappropriate analysis of variance.

SIDNEY
In this case that's true. It seems that the analysis of variance is robust indeed! In other examples, the two approaches will, however, often lead to different conclusions and it's clear that a method assuming normality is incorrect.

FRANCES
Something we haven't looked at yet is those mothers who fail to complete the study. I think it's important to try to discover the factors that cause mothers to drop out. In particular, I would like to know whether there is a different drop-out pattern in the various treatment groups. At the moment I've simply counted the number of drop-outs in each group and calculated a chi-square (see Display 8.8).

Display 8.8 Number of Drop-Outs by Treatment Group

Dropout	Group				Total
	1	2	3	4	
Yes	7	2	5	3	17
No	8	13	10	12	43

Chi-Square = 4.84;   d.f. = 3; $p = 0.18$

SIDNEY

Again, we can begin by using logistic regression with the dichotomous dependent variable now dropping out—yes or no. Apart from treatment group, what are the other variables that you think might influence whether or not a woman drops out of the treatment programme?

FRANCES

Again marital conflict might be important. For example, it's possible that the family therapy treatment actually provokes conflict between the woman and her husband, at least in the short run. Alternatively, maybe the husband himself is difficult and demanding and needs a lot of care, which detracts from the family's ability to participate in the treatment programme. We don't have measures of the husband's personality and behaviour but we do know whether or not he has suffered from a psychiatric illness in the past. That might be important. And, finally, we need to consider the actual relationship between mother and child during the treatment programme. If they have a very good relationship and the mother usually enjoys the baby, she may see no need to stay in the treatment programme. I think the two observational ratings of emotional closeness between mother and child would get at this dimension.

SIDNEY

The husband's psychiatric history is a categorical variable with two categories and raises no new problems. Using the two ratings of emotional closeness could cause problems because they are likely to be rather highly correlated.

FRANCES

Why should this be a problem?

SIDNEY

Well, the interpretation of regression coefficients becomes less straightforward. You may recall from our previous discussion (see Chapter 6) that such coefficients can be interpreted as the change in the response variable produced by a unit change in the corresponding *explanatory* or *independent* variable when all other explanatory variables are held constant. Clearly, this interpretation becomes problematical when there are substantial correlations between the explanatory variables. In this case it makes little sense to talk of changing one of the ratings of emotional closeness, whilst keeping the other constant. And, on a more technical note,

---

Display 8.9 Logistic Model for Drop-outs

Term	Coeff.	SE	Coeff./SE
CD	0.07	0.64	0.11
FT	−1.17	0.65	−1.80
HP	0.63	0.82	0.76
Conflict	0.19	0.19	1.00
EC	−0.07	0.17	−0.39

Comparing each coefficient divided by the appropriate standard error, with the 5% normal deviate, 1.96, shows that none of the coefficients are significantly different from zero although that for family therapy approaches significance. The negative sign of the coefficient indicates that the number of drop-outs *decreases* from the no-family-therapy condition (coded 0) to family therapy received (coded 1).

---

highly correlated explanatory variables can lead to numerical difficulties in certain matrix operations involved in the regression calculations.

FRANCES
So should I simply drop one of the ratings?

SIDNEY
That's one obvious solution, another is simply to take the average of the two ratings. For now let's simply use only the first value.

FRANCES
So now we can go ahead with the logistic regression?

SIDNEY
We can indeed. First let's consider the regression coefficients that arise when all your explanatory variables are included in the analysis (see Display 8.9). It seems that none of your variables have a dramatic effect on the chance of a mother dropping out of the study, although there is some evidence that dropping out is less of a problem for the mothers receiving family therapy.

FRANCES
Well, that has given me some insights into what causes mothers to drop out of the study, information that may be extremely useful in future studies. There is, however, a further question I have about drop-outs and that is about the amount of time they stay in the study before they drop out. Again, I would like to know which of my explanatory variables have an effect on the duration of time spent in the study.

SIDNEY
Here, of course, the most straightforward analysis would be simply to consider the subset of mothers who did drop out of the study, and regress time in the study on the explanatory variables of interest (see Display

Display 8.10 Regression Analysis of Time to Dropout for Mothers not Completing 24 Weeks

Term	Coeff.	SE	Coeff/SE
CD	0.43	2.71	0.16
FT	−3.59	3.23	−1.11
Conflict	−0.43	1.15	−0.37
EC	1.11	0.85	1.30
HP	−4.67	3.21	−1.45

8.10). Such an analysis does, however, have an obvious problem. Can you think what it is?

FRANCES

Well one thing that does concern me is that it disregards the information from mothers who stay in the study for the whole 24 weeks. If, for example, the study had been of 36 weeks' duration, it's reasonable to assume there would have been more drop-outs, so I don't think we can assume that mothers who remain for 24 weeks would never have dropped out—essentially the 24 weeks is arbitrary.

8.3   Survival Analysis

SIDNEY

That's right. Such data, where we measure the time to some event but where for some individuals the event does not happen before the study ends, are best dealt with by some methods known collectively as *survival analysis*. For the mothers who do not drop out in the 24 weeks of the study, the assumption is made that the only thing known about the time they would take to drop out is that it is greater than 24 weeks. Making such an assumption allows all the observations to be considered, even those from the women who completed the study. The effects of covariates on the chance of dropping out can now be studied by another form of regression—*Cox's regression* or the *proportional hazard model*. Here it is the *hazard function* which is modelled.

FRANCES

I'm afraid I have no idea what a hazard function is.

SIDNEY

Essentially, this function is a measure of how likely an individual is to experience the event of interest as a function of time. In your case, we are asking how likely a mother is to drop out, as a function of the time she has already been in the study. The hazard function may remain constant, increase, decrease or involve some more complex process. Rather than spend time on the details of the method (see Display 8.11), let's apply it to your data and see how to interpret the results (see Display 8.12).

Display 8.11 The Proportional Hazards Model

To introduce the basic concepts suppose we have only two explanatory variables x_1 and x_2 which do not vary with time. A first step in the modelling process might be to assume that the hazard function, $h(t)$, is a linear function of x_1 and x_2. Such a model could however lead to problems since $h(t)$ is restricted to being positive but this restriction is not built into the proposed model (cf. logistic regression). Consequently a more sensible model would involve a linear model for the *natural logarithm* of the hazard function—the simplest possibility would be

$$\ln h(t) = \alpha + \beta_1 x_1 + \beta_2 x_2$$

where α, β_1 and β_2 are parameters which must be estimated. In this simple model the hazard function does not depend on time and this is clearly very restrictive.

The proportional hazards model assumes that the hazard function does depend on time but avoids specifying the form of the dependence by assuming the model

$$\ln h(t) = \alpha(t) + \beta_1 x_1 + \beta_2 x_2$$

where $\alpha(t)$ is an arbitrary function of time. The term "proportional hazards" arises because for any two individuals at any point in time the ratio of their hazards is a constant. Because the baseline hazard function, $\alpha(t)$, does not have to be specified explicitly, the proportional hazards model is essentially *non-parametric*.

Display 8.12 Proportional Hazards Model for Drop-outs

Term	Coeff.	SE	Coeff/SE	Exp(coeff)
CD	0.074	0.513	0.144	1.076
FT	−0.856	0.538	−1.59	0.424
Conflict	0.130	0.159	0.818	1.139
EC	−0.063	0.143	−0.443	0.938
HP	0.486	0.684	0.711	1.626

The only coefficient that approaches being significant is that for family therapy. If we simply assume all the other coefficients are actually zero, then the model becomes (remember that no family therapy is scored 1 and family therapy 2)

(1)   No Family Therapy

$$\ln h(t) = \alpha(t) - 0.856 \times 1$$

(2)   Family Therapy

$$\ln h(t) = \alpha(t) - 0.856 \times 2$$

Therefore, the difference in log hazard functions, i.e., the log of the ratio of the hazards, is -0.856. Exponentiating this gives 0.42, so the hazard of dropping out for those mothers receiving family therapy is 42% of that for the mothers not receiving this treatment. In other words mothers not receiving family therapy are about twice as likely to drop out at any stage as those receiving family therapy.

9

Fitting Models of Relationships Amongst Variables

9.1 Introduction

As we mentioned in the first chapter, there has recently been a conceptual revolution in psychology that derives from innovations in statistical theory and associated computer software. There are now some more or less agreed-upon procedures for making causal inferences from non-experimental data. These involve the specification of latent variables and the use of structural equation models of their associations. A complete review of such procedures is beyond the scope of this book; however, the psychological researcher needs to become at least minimally acquainted with the logic and procedures involved. More and more researchers are applying such methods, and so the average psychologist needs to become familiar with some guidelines for the interpretation of findings from such studies, if only to be an informed consumer of other people's research.

In this chapter, Frances and Sidney discuss some model-fitting procedures that can be applied to the long-term findings from the prevention programme.

FRANCES
Well, here I am at long last with some data from the follow-up phase of my prevention study. I now have information about the children at the age of three, both in terms of their IQ scores and their ratings on the behaviour problems checklist. With respect to the latter, I have tallied the scores on the aggression and depression scales, and also indicated whether an individual child's score meets the criterion for psychiatric caseness on that scale. In other words, I have continuous measures of tendencies to

aggressive and depressive behaviour and counts of children who meet the diagnostic criteria to be considered clinically aggressive or depressed.

Obviously, I want to determine the extent to which the children's outcomes are determined by the experimental treatments, which, as you recall, included consultation with a child development specialist and/or participation in family therapy. But, as the years have gone by, I have become convinced that it would be useful to try to get some overall measure of family risk to use as a covariate in such analyses. In other words, I have measured such things as the father's psychiatric history, the degree of marital conflict, the mother's dysphoria during the postnatal period, and so on. Perhaps none of these measures individually mediates the impact of the prevention programme on the child's eventual academic potential and behaviour. But I would like to explore some relationships amongst these risk variables in the early part of the study and then perhaps examine the relationship of a composite measure with the later outcomes.

I think I would like to start by examining the relationships amongst different pieces of information about the family system: the father's psychiatric history; the degree of marital conflict during the early part of the study; the level of the mother's dysphoria during the early part of the study, perhaps in terms of mean ratings or perhaps in terms of the categorical variable of whether she was diagnosed as clinically depressed; and something about the actual qualities of the mother–infant relationship in the first months of the child's life. I think I might take use the emotional closeness ratings and time spent in direct interaction to estimate the latter. Can I use both continuous and categorical variables in such an analysis? Am I talking about some form of factor analysis?

9.2   Factor Analysis

SIDNEY

Factor analysis is a term used to cover a variety of techniques which try to make sense of complex *multivariate data.* In very general terms these methods try to find an explanation for the correlations between a set of observed variables in terms of a small number of underlying *latent variables* which can't be measured directly.

Latent variables occur in many areas: for example, in psychology, such concepts as *intelligence* and *verbal ability,* in sociology, *ambition* and *racial prejudice* and in economics, *economic expectation.* Clearly, direct measurement of an internal concept such as racial prejudice is not possible. One could, however, observe whether a person approves or disapproves of a particular piece of government legislation on racial equality, and whether or not she numbers members of a particular race among her friends and acquaintances, etc., and assume that these two variables are, in some sense, *indicators* of the more fundamental variable, *racial prejudice.*

Factor analysis methods are used for investigating the dependence of the set of observed variables on a small number of latent variables. Let's begin by having a look at a very simple example which involves a naive

---

Display 9.1 A Simple Factor Analysis Model

Spearman (1904) considered children's examination marks in three sub-jects, classics (x_1), French (x_2) and English (x_3) and found the following correlations:

$$
\begin{array}{c}
\\
x_1 \\
x_2 \\
x_3
\end{array}
\begin{array}{ccc}
x_1 & x_2 & x_3 \\
\left(\begin{array}{ccc}
1.00 & & \\
0.83 & 1.00 & \\
0.78 & 0.67 & 1.00
\end{array} \right)
\end{array}
$$

Here it might be assumed that a single latent variable, *general intelligence*, underlies the data and the corresponding factor model would be

$$x_1 = \lambda_1 f + u_1$$
$$x_2 = \lambda_2 f + u_2$$
$$x_3 = \lambda_3 f + u_3$$

where λ_1, λ_2 and λ_3 are regression coefficients for each observed variable on factor, f, and u_1, u_2 and u_3 represent random disturbance terms.

In the factor analysis context the λ_i are more commonly referred to as *factor loadings*, f is known as a *common factor* and the u_i as *specific factors*.

In this example the common factor, f, might be equated with intelligence or general intellectual ability, and the specific factors, u_i, will have small variances if the corresponding observed variable is closely related to f. In theory the variation in u_i could be partioned into two parts. The first would represent the extent to which an individual's ability at classics, say, differs from his general intellectual ability; the second would represent the fact that the examination is only an approximate measure of ability in the particular subject. In practice this distinction is usually ignored.

---

attempt to measure the latent variable, intelligence (see Display 9.1). In general, of course, the model is a little more involved (see Display 9.2).

Let's look at what happens when we apply a particular factor analysis procedure, principal components analysis, to the variables in your study that measure various aspects of the families. To simplify the analysis I have taken the mean of the available monthly dysphoria scores as a measure of a woman's overall dysphoria, and also averaged the two ratings you have for emotional closeness and those for duration of mother child interaction. The results look quite interesting (see Display 9.3).

The analysis has identified two factors; the first seems to reflect the ex-perience of motherhood, being a contrast between the mother's dysphoria and the quality of her relationship with her child. The second appears to be a measure of the nature of the woman's marriage.

FRANCES
The factor analysis does seem to have turned up something quite interesting and useful. It suggests that a woman's feelings on becoming a mother, and the nature of the relationship with her baby, are relatively independent of her experience of marriage. Perhaps that doesn't bode too well for the

---

Display 9.2 The Common Factor Model

The general form of the factor analysis model postulates that the manifest variables, $x_1, x_2, \ldots, x_p$, are linear functions of the latent variables plus an error or residual term:

$$x_1 = \lambda_{11}f_1 + \lambda_{12}f_2 + \cdots + \lambda_{1k}f_k + u_1,$$
$$x_2 = \lambda_{21}f_1 + \lambda_{22}f_2 + \cdots + \lambda_{2k}f_k + u_2,$$
$$\vdots$$
$$x_p = \lambda_{p1}f_1 + \lambda_{p2}f_2 + \cdots + \lambda_{pk}f_k + u_p$$

where $f_1, f_2, \ldots, f_k$ represent the k latent variables or *common factors*, $u_1, u_2, \ldots, u_p$ represent the residual terms—i.e. the combined effects of *specific factors* and random error—and the λ_{ij} the standardised regression coefficients of manifest on latent variables. These coefficients are generally known as *factor loadings*.

The factor analysis model implies that the covariance matrix of the observed variables, Σ, has the following form:

$$\Sigma = \Lambda\Lambda' + \Psi$$

where Λ is a $p \times k$ matrix of factor loadings and Ψ is a $p \times p$ diagonal matrix the diagonal elements of which contain the variances of the residual terms in the factor analysis model.

The aim of any factor analysis model is to estimate a loading matrix and a diagonal matrix of unique variances so that the covariance matrix of the observed variables is reproduced as closely as possible by the above equation.

The most commonly used methods are *principal factor analysis*, and *maximum likelihood factor analysis*. A related technique is *principal components analysis*, which seeks linear functions of the observed variables which are uncorrelated with one another and account for maximal amounts of the observed variables variance. A detailed account of all methods is given in Everitt and Dunn(1991).

---

marriage! **What I would like to do now is to get a score for each woman on each of the two factors and then compare these scores for the depressed and non-depressed women. How would I go about this?**

SIDNEY

There are a variety of ways of obtaining factor scores, some complicated and some simple. For our purpose, a simple approach is probably quite sufficient (see Display 9.4). Let's now look at the summary statistics of the two derived scores for your four treatment groups (see Display 9.5).

On the first factor, high positive scores are obviously "good" since they imply above-average scores on emotional closeness and duration of mother–child interaction. For the second factor, low or negative scores are desirable since they correspond to lower than average scores on marital conflict and to a husband who does not have a psychiatric history.

Display 9.3 Factor Analysis of Family Variables

Correlation Matrix

$$R = \begin{array}{r} \\ \text{Dysph} \\ \text{Mcemot} \\ \text{Mcdur} \\ \text{Conflict} \\ \text{HP} \end{array} \begin{pmatrix} \text{Dysph} & \text{Mcemot} & \text{Mcdur} & \text{Conflict} & \text{HP} \\ 1.00 \\ -0.44 & 1.00 \\ -0.41 & 0.62 & 1.00 \\ 0.33 & -0.25 & -0.33 & 1.00 \\ 0.052 & -0.319 & -0.18 & 0.57 & 1.00 \end{pmatrix}$$

The factor loadings are as follows:

	f_1	f_2
Dysph	−0.768	0.040
Mcemot	0.803	−0.226
Mcdur	0.823	−0.161
Conflict	−0.265	0.821
HP	−0.044	0.918

These two factors account for 71% of the variance in the original five variables.

Display 9.4 Calculating Factor Scores

In Frances' example we can calculate factor scores simply by combining the scores of the manifest variables in accordance with the factor loadings. We must remember however that we need to deal with *standard scores*. So, for example, the f_1 score (experience of motherhood) may be calculated as

$$F_1 = \frac{\text{Mcemot} - 4.92}{1.59} + \frac{\text{Mcdur} - 33.95}{10.82} - \frac{\text{Dysph} - 3.87}{1.59}$$

(Conflict and husbands psychiatric history have been ignored and the actual loadings replaced by "ones" with the appropriate sign.)

Scores on factor two (quality of marriage) are given by

$$F_2 = \frac{\text{Conflict} - 4.43}{2.19} + \frac{\text{HP} - 0.18}{0.38}$$

FRANCES

Having identified the underlying variables generating the relationships between my family variables, I would now like to go on and investigate how these factors and my treatment variables affect the child's outcome. I am interested in two general outcomes—the child's intellectual attainment, as measured by the IQ test, and any behavioural and emotional problems the child might have, as measured by the behaviour problems checklist. I am

Display 9.5 Summary Statistics on Factor Scores for the Four Treatment Groups

Factor 1

		CD	
		No	Yes
FT	No	−0.62	0.56
	Yes	−0.20	0.25

Factor 2

		CD	
		No	Yes
FT	No	1.14	−0.35
	Yes	−0.17	0.48

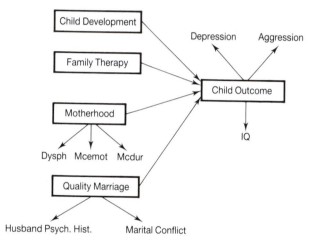

Display 9.6   Path Diagram for Child Outcome Model

particularly interested in the two scores derived from the checklist—the aggression score and the depression score.

9.3   Modelling Latent Variables

SIDNEY

It sounds as though you want to look at a specific model for your data which includes the effect of latent variables and observed variables on other latent variables. The model I think you have in mind is illustrated in this *path diagram* (see Display 9.6).

FRANCES

Yes, I think that's correct.

SIDNEY

Such a model makes a specific prediction for the correlations between your observed variables in terms of the parameters of the model. In other

Display 9.7 A Simple Example of A Latent Variable Model

Consider a simple example in which there are two latent variables, u and v, and two observed variables, x and y, related as follows:

$$x = u + \delta$$
$$y = v + \epsilon$$

where δ and ϵ represent some form of measurement error.

Suppose we have a further observed variable which is also related to the latent variable u as follows:

$$z = u + \gamma$$

If we assume that δ, γ and ϵ have zero means, that δ and γ are uncorrelated with each other and with u and that ϵ is uncorrelated with v, then the covariance matrix of the three observed variables, x, y and z, may be expressed in terms of parameters representing the variances and covariances of the errors of measurement and of the latent variables, to give

$$\begin{pmatrix} \text{Var}(y) & & \\ \text{Cov}(x,y) & \text{Var}(x) & \\ \text{Cov}(z,y) & \text{Cov}(z,x) & \text{Var}(z) \end{pmatrix} = \begin{pmatrix} \theta_1 + \theta_2 & & \\ \theta_3 & \theta_4 + \theta_5 & \\ \theta_3 & \theta_4 & \theta_4 + \theta_6 \end{pmatrix}$$

where

$\theta_1 = \text{Var}(v), \theta_2 = \text{Var}(\epsilon), \theta_3 = \text{Cov}(v, u), \theta_4 = \text{Var}(u), \theta_5 = \text{Var}(\delta),$

$\theta_6 = \text{Var}(\gamma)$

By equating corresponding terms and solving the resulting series of simultaneous equations, estimates of the parameters might be obtained in terms of the variances and covariances of the observed variables.

In this example however we could not get unique estimates of θ_1 and θ_2—one can be increased by some amount and the other decreased by the same amount without altering the predicted covariance matrix. The model is said to be *unidentified*, which simply means that *unique* parameter estimates are not available.

words, each of the observed correlations will, according to your model, be specific, and possibly complicated, functions of the regression coefficients, factor loadings and unique variances. Perhaps an explanation in terms of a very simple example would help (see Display 9.7).

To fit the model, we choose the various parameter estimates to make the predicted correlations as close as possible to those observed. The details are not important but essentially we begin with some "guess" at the parameter values and then proceed to adjust these values to make the observed and predicted correlations or covariances correspond more closely (see Display 9.8). More important is to know how to interpret these estimates and how to assess the fit of the model (see Display 9.9).

FRANCES
I'm rather confused as to why one of the loadings for the child outcome

---

Display 9.8 Estimating the Parameters in Latent Variable Models

Such models imply a particular form for the population covariance matrix of the manifest variables, in the sense that the elements of this matrix are particular functions of the parameters of the model. Estimates of the parameters are obtained by minimising some function of the discrepancy between the observed covariance matrix, **S**, and that predicted by the model, $\hat{\mathbf{\Sigma}}$. One such function is the sum of squares of the differences between corresponding elements of **S** and $\hat{\mathbf{\Sigma}}$.

The goodness of fit of a model can be judged in a variety of ways, the most common being by a chi-square statistic and by the *residual correlations*, i.e. the differences between the observed values and those values predicted by the model.

Display 9.9 Some Parameter Estimates and their Standard Errors for Frances' Model

The estimated coefficients relating the two treatment variables to child outcome and their standard errors are

(1)   Child Development—Coefficient=0.037, Standard Error=0.088.
(2)   Family Therapy—Coefficient=0.098, Standard Error=0.091.

The estimated coefficients for motherhood and quality of marriage are
(1)   Motherhood—Coefficient=0.449, Standard Error=0.150
(2)   Quality of Marriage—Coefficient=0.127, Standard Error=0.094

The estimated loadings for the motherhood latent variable are:
(1)   Dysphoria—Coefficient=−0.578, Standard Error=0.151
(2)   Emotional Closeness—Coefficient=0.805, Standard Error=0.142
(3)   Duration—Coefficient=0.754, Standard Error=0.144

The estimated loadings for the quality of marriage latent variable are:
(1)   Marital Conflict—Coefficient=0.616, Standard Error=0.134
(2)   Husband's Psychiatric History—Coefficient=1.000, Standard Error=0.105

The estimated loadings on the child outcome latent variable are:
(1)   Child IQ—Coefficient=1.000 (This value is fixed to set the scale of the latent variable—see Everitt, 1984 for details)
(2)   Child Depression—Coefficient=−1.186, Standard Error=0.469
(3)   Child Aggression—Coefficient=0.268, Standard Error=0.349

The chi-square goodness-of-fit measure takes the value 56.61 with 33 d.f. corresponding to a *p*-value of 0.006. Clearly the proposed model does not provide a very good prediction of the observed correlations.

---

latent variable has been set to a value of one, since this hasn't been done for the motherhood and quality of marriage latent variables.

SIDNEY
This is rather confusing, but it arises because we need to set a scale for each latent variable before we can set about estimating the parameters of interest. One way to do this is simply to assume that the latent variables are standard scores and that therefore their variance is one. Another possibility is to *fix* one of the loadings, usually to one, which then sets the scale of the latent variable to that of the corresponding observed variable. In the case of the motherhood and quality of marriage variables I've used the first approach and for the child's outcome I've used the second.

It appears that the largest influence on the child's outcome is produced by the motherhood latent variable. The coefficients for the effect of quality of marriage and the two treatments are not significantly different from zero. The model tells us that an increase in positive feelings about motherhood increases the value of the child outcome variable, an increase in the latter being associated with an increase in child IQ and/or a decrease in child depression.

FRANCES
Unfortunately the overall model doesn't seem to fit very well.

SIDNEY
It certainly seems that there are factors other than those you've investigated that affect child outcome. To improve the fit you would need to search for additional predictor variables. But the model is helpful I think, in separating out which of the variables you *have* considered that are important in determining what happens to the child.

References

Arbuthnott, J. (1710), An argument for divine providence, taken from the constant regularity observed in the births of both sexes. *Philosophical Transactions,* **27**, 186–190.

Cliff, N. (1983), Some cautions concerning the application of causal modelling methods. *Multiv. Behav. Res.,* **18**, 115–126.

Coghill, S., Caplan, H., Alexandra, H., Robson, K., and Kumar, R. (1986), Impact of post natal depression on cognitive development in young children. *Br. Med. J.,* **292**, 1165–1167.

Cronbach, L. (1957), The two disciplines of scientific psychology. *American Psychologist,* **12**, 671–684.

Crutchfield, R.S. (1938), Efficient factorial design and analysis of variance illustrated in psychological experimentation, *J. of Psychology,* **5**, 339–346.

Crutchfield, R.S. (1939), The determiners of energy expenditure in string-pulling by the rat, *J. of Psychology,* **7**, 163–178.

Crutchfield, R.S. and Tolman, E.C. (1940), Multiple variable design for experiments involving interaction of behaviour, *Psych. Rev.,* **47**, 38–42.

Dunn, G. (1989), *Design and Analysis of Reliability Studies,* Edward Arnold, London.

Edgeworth, F.Y. (1885), *Methods of statistics,* Jubilee Volume of the Statistical Society.

Emerson, J.D., and Stoto, M.A. (1983). Transforming Data, In *Understanding Robust and Exploratory Data Analysis* (Eds., D.C. Hoaglin, F. Mosteller, and J.W. Tukey), John Wiley and Sons, New York.

Everitt, B.S. (1984). *An Introduction to Latent Variable Models,* Chapman and Hall, London.

Everitt, B.S. and Dunn, G. (1991), *Applied Multivariate Data Analysis.* Edward Arnold, Sevenoaks.

Fleiss, J.L. (1986), *The Design and Analysis of Clinical Experiments,* John Wiley and Sons, New York.

Gardner, M.J. and Altman, D.G. (1986), Confidence intervals rather than p values: estimation rather than hypothesis testing. *Br. Med. J.,* **292**, 746–750.

Gaskill, H.V. and Cox, G.M. (1937), Patterns in emotional reactions 1. Respiration: the use of analysis of variance and covariance in psychological data. *J. of General Psychology,* **16**, 21–38.

Greenhouse, S.W. and Geisser, S. (1959), On methods in the analysis of profile data. *Psychometrika,* **24**, 95–112.

Huynh, H., and Feldt, L.S. (1970), Conditions under which mean square ratios in repeated measurement designs have exact F-distributions. *J. Am. Statist. Assoc.,* **65**, 1582–1589.

Huynh, H., and Feldt, L.S. (1980), Performance of traditional F tests in repeated measures designs under covariance heterogeneity. *Communications in Statistics—Theory and Methods,* **A9**, 61–74.

Krzanowski, W.J. (1988), *Principles of Multivariate Analysis.* Oxford Science Publications.

Landis, J.R. and Koch, G.C. (1977), The measurement of observer agreement for categorical data. *Biometrics*, **33**, 159–174.

Little, R.A. and Rubin, D.B. (1987), *Statistical Analysis with Missing Data*, John Wiley and Sons, New York.

Lovie, A.D. (1979), The analysis of variance in experimental psychology 1934–1945, *Brit. J. Math. and Stat. Psychol.*, **32**, 151–178.

Mitchell, J. (1767), An inquiry into the probable parallax and magnitude of the fixed stars, from the quantity of light which they afford us and the particular circumstances of their situation. *Phil. Trans. Roy. Soc.*, London, 87.

Nelder, J.A. and McCullagh, P. (1990), *Generalized Linear Models*, 2nd Ed., Chapman and Hall, London.

Oakes M.L. (1979), The Statistical Evaluation of Psychological Evidence. Unpublished doctoral thesis, University of Hull.

Oakes M. (1986), *Statistical Inference: a Commentary for the Social and Behavioural Sciences*, John Wiley and Sons, Chichester.

Scheffé, H.A. (1953), A method for judging all possible contrasts in the analysis of variance, *Biometrika*, **40**, 87–104.

Singer, B. (1979), Distribution–free methods for non-parametric problems: A classified and selected bibliography. *Br. J. Math. Statist. Psychol.*, **32**, 1–60.

Skipper, J.K., Guenther, A.L. and Naso, G. (1967). The sacredness of 0.05; a note concerning the use of statistical levels of significance in social science, *The American Psychologist*, **1**, 16–18.

Spearman, C. (1904), 'General Intelligence' objectively determined and measured. *Am. J. Psychol.*, **15**, 201–293.

Sprent, P. (1970), Some problems of statistical consultancy, *J. Roy. Statist. Soc.*, A, **133**, 139–165.

Sterling T.D. (1959), Publications decisions and their possible effects on inferences drawn from tests of significance—or vice versa. *J. Am. Statist. Assoc.*, **54**, 30–34.

Tukey, J.W. (1972), Some graphic and semigraphic displays. In *Statistical Papers in Honor of George W. Swedecor* (Ed. T.A. Bancroft), Iowa State University Press, Iowa.

Tukey, J.W. (1977), *Exploratory Data Analysis*, Addison Wesley, Reading, Massachusetts.

Winer, B.J. (1971), *Statistical Principles in Experimental Design*, McGraw-Hill, New York.

APPENDIX
Data Sets

Appendix A

IQ and Depression Data

					VARIABLES						
1	2	3	4	5	6	7	8	9	10	11	12
2	1	1	103	56	50	49	50	42	4	0	1
4	1	1	124	65	56	51	64	61	12	0	15
6	1	1	124	67	59	55	61	63	9	0	7
7	1	2	104	52	49	52	55	44	3	0	5
8	2	2	96	46	35	46	52	46	3	0	8
9	1	1	92	46	23	45	43	43	3	0	6
12	1	2	124	58	49	65	68	65	6	0	5
14	1	2	99	55	52	45	46	50	4	0	9
15	1	1	92	46	36	46	41	55	3	0	6
16	1	1	116	61	50	51	58	51	9	0	2
17	1	1	99	58	49	43	45	50	11	0	3
18	2	2	22	22	22	22	50	22	17	1	6
19	2	2	81	47	49	34	38	41	6	1	2
20	1	2	117	68	58	52	53	63	7	0	7
22	2	2	100	54	56	41	47	53	10	1	13
23	1	2	89	48	33	49	41	46	11	0	14
25	1	2	125	64	47	67	66	67	9	0	7
26	1	1	127	64	55	64	68	71	9	1	4
27	1	2	112	50	46	57	57	64	5	0	7
29	1	2	48	23	24	20	20	25	9	0	5
30	1	1	139	68	59	56	75	64	2	0	3
31	1	2	118	58	46	55	64	61	8	0	3
33	2	2	107	45	40	56	58	58	5	1	14
34	1	1	106	46	40	54	57	53	0	0	4
35	2	1	129	63	50	71	70	67	4	0	2
36	1	1	117	43	42	65	71	63	5	0	4
37	1	1	123	64	64	57	64	61	2	1	4
38	1	2	118	64	49	56	56	60	4	0	6
39	2	1	84	47	42	41	37	43	10	1	4
40	1	1	117	66	59	51	64	61	2	0	4
41	2	2	101	48	46	48	52	52	6	0	2
42	1	1	141	66	56	69	76	69	4	0	1
44	1	1	124	60	58	62	77	58	7	0	4
46	1	1	110	50	42	66	61	52	7	0	3
47	1	1	98	54	58	45	47	48	3	0	10
48	1	2	109	64	54	45	48	50	9	0	4
50	1	1	120	71	68	53	53	63	10	0	5
53	1	1	127	67	62	62	68	59	6	0	4
54	1	2	103	55	50	46	52	48	6	0	2
56	1	1	118	65	55	49	57	61	5	0	5
57	1	1	117	60	51	55	64	48	5	0	9
59	1	1	115	52	52	63	67	55	7	0	5
60	1	1	119	63	52	55	62	58	4	0	6
62	1	1	117	63	53	56	56	59	4	0	3
63	1	1	92	45	44	39	42	55	7	0	5
65	1	2	101	53	41	46	48	52	10	0	5
66	1	1	119	59	53	58	65	59	2	0	7
68	1	1	144	78	73	67	67	65	3	0	7
69	1	1	119	66	59	54	54	62	5	0	9

					VARIABLES (continued)						
1	2	3	4	5	6	7	8	9	10	11	12
71	1	1	127	67	60	68	63	67	7	0	4
73	1	2	113	61	48	48	54	58	7	0	6
75	1	1	127	60	61	64	59	68	2	0	6
77	1	1	103	57	49	56	50	48	3	0	9
78	1	2	128	70	70	62	65	60	8	0	6
79	1	2	86	45	35	38	45	28	7	0	3
80	1	1	112	62	58	50	51	60	10	0	4
81	1	2	115	59	46	58	58	59	4	0	6
82	1	2	117	48	50	56	68	62	11	0	6
83	1	2	99	58	51	44	48	41	3	0	4
85	1	2	110	54	51	58	61	47	4	0	10
86	2	2	139	70	66	62	72	66	6	0	5
87	1	2	117	64	53	64	57	51	4	0	4
89	1	1	96	52	45	46	45	47	5	0	8
90	2	1	111	54	49	54	60	50	5	0	5
91	1	1	118	58	54	60	62	64	4	0	3
92	1	1	126	66	59	60	64	67	11	0	4
94	1	2	126	69	67	61	66	55	2	0	2
95	1	2	89	49	44	40	36	36	10	0	3
96	1	1	102	56	51	42	49	50	4	0	5
97	1	1	134	74	70	56	68	59	5	0	5
98	1	1	93	47	67	46	46	45	5	0	10
99	1	1	115	55	52	51	61	60	1	0	5
100	2	2	99	50	41	49	48	54	13	1	4
101	1	2	99	58	57	41	44	47	8	0	9
102	1	2	122	55	53	70	64	74	0	0	6
103	1	2	106	49	48	48	54	59	5	1	9
104	1	2	124	66	54	63	58	68	1	0	6
106	1	1	100	43	45	56	56	48	4	0	4
107	1	1	114	61	54	55	56	55	7	0	11
108	1	1	121	64	61	60	66	50	1	0	6
109	1	1	119	63	56	65	61	60	5	0	4
110	1	1	108	48	49	54	60	50	4	0	3
111	1	1	110	66	58	44	56	48	10	0	5
112	1	1	127	62	65	58	71	61	4	0	3
113	1	2	118	66	53	60	56	58	2	0	3
115	1	2	107	53	40	58	54	52	3	0	5
116	2	2	123	62	57	65	68	59	2	0	3
117	2	2	102	48	45	52	52	58	5	0	5
119	1	2	110	65	60	50	47	55	6	1	7
120	1	1	114	64	56	51	56	47	4	0	5
121	1	2	118	58	51	62	63	52	2	0	5
123	2	1	101	44	41	54	56	47	7	0	9
124	2	1	121	64	48	62	62	62	6	0	5
127	1	2	114	50	36	55	65	51	2	0	6

1 = Subject ID
2 = Depression at three months
   (1 = no, 2 = yes)
3 = sex of child (1 = Boys, 2 = Girls)
4 = IQ
5 = Perceptual
6 = Motor
7 = Memory

8 = Verbal
9 = Quantitative
10 = Behavioural Problems
11 = Husband's psychiatric history
   (0 = none, 1 = has previous
   psychiatric history)
12 = Birth hazards score

Appendix B

Data from Longitudinal Study

	1	2	3	4	5	6	7	8	9	10	11	12	13	14	15	16	17	18	19	20	21	22	23	24	25	26	27	28
																			VARIABLES									
1	1	1	1	4	4	5	4	6	6	8	9	5	6	7	7	1	15	22	3	4	98	6	0	40	0	8	1	24
2	2	1	1	1	3	5	2	2	4	2	5	2	2	3	3	0	35	20	5	5	101	2	0	50	1	8	1	24
3	3	1	1	3	7	8	8	7	-9	-9	-9	-9	-9	-9	-9	1	10	7	2	2	98	11	0	35	0	5	0	22
4	4	1	1	7	5	8	8	8	9	9	-9	-9	-9	-9	-9	1	40	10	6	9	86	3	0	43	0	7	1	10
5	5	1	1	5	5	2	2	2	4	4	5	4	2	4	2	0	47	34	6	7	105	13	0	30	0	4	0	24
6	6	1	1	2	2	6	6	6	8	8	-9	-9	-9	-9	-9	1	12	18	2	2	86	4	1	9	-9	7	0	16
7	7	1	1	8	4	5	7	7	9	9	9	-9	-9	-9	-9	1	12	-9	3	-9	115	-9	0	44	-9	7	0	14
8	8	1	1	5	2	2	3	2	1	1	2	2	2	3	3	1	26	57	7	7	-9	9	-9	-9	-9	5	1	24
9	9	1	1	7	4	4	4	7	9	9	9	9	9	9	9	1	39	44	7	8	-9	5	-9	39	-9	6	0	20
10	10	1	1	4	3	6	3	4	4	3	3	3	3	3	3	0	45	30	0	0	101	2	0	25	0	2	1	24
11	11	1	1	6	4	3	3	6	-9	-9	-9	-9	-9	-9	-9	0	36	50	1	1	121	11	0	33	0	7	0	20
12	12	2	1	3	3	4	4	8	8	4	7	7	7	7	7	0	44	15	5	7	106	4	0	26	1	5	0	24
13	13	2	1	4	6	6	6	9	3	3	2	2	2	2	2	0	25	34	4	2	96	7	0	52	-9	7	0	24
14	14	2	1	6	3	3	3	3	9	9	9	9	9	9	9	0	41	50	3	6	90	6	0	42	0	8	0	4
15	15	2	1	3	6	4	4	4	3	5	2	2	2	2	2	0	20	9	3	2	102	7	0	55	-9	4	1	21
16	16	2	2	5	6	4	4	8	4	1	1	1	1	1	1	0	25	38	5	5	98	6	0	42	0	3	0	24
17	17	2	2	5	6	6	8	2	-9	-9	-9	-9	-9	-9	-9	0	55	46	7	4	110	5	0	55	-9	3	0	24
18	18	2	2	2	5	6	3	5	5	5	9	9	9	9	7	0	55	20	7	5	80	4	0	23	0	8	0	20
19	19	2	1	5	2	2	4	5	4	5	2	2	2	2	2	1	48	30	3	4	118	4	0	38	0	4	0	24
20	20	2	1	3	4	2	8	2	5	4	1	1	1	1	1	0	22	10	2	5	-9	-9	0	23	0	3	0	24
21	21	2	2	4	6	2	3	5	-9	-9	-9	-9	-9	-9	-9	0	38	44	6	5	125	2	0	33	0	5	1	20
22	22	2	2	6	3	5	5	1	3	3	9	9	9	9	9	0	23	37	7	2	101	15	0	15	0	7	0	24
23	23	2	2	5	5	5	2	3	4	2	3	3	3	3	3	0	17	31	5	6	98	3	0	20	0	5	0	16
24	24	1	2	2	4	4	6	3	-9	-9	-9	-9	-9	-9	-9	0	40	44	5	7	112	9	0	37	0	3	0	24
25	25	2	2	5	4	3	2	1	2	2	1	1	1	1	1	0	27	-9	4	5	99	7	0	25	0	5	0	24
26	26	2	2	2	5	5	5	3	4	4	9	9	9	9	9	1	20	35	8	2	105	3	0	26	0	5	0	24
27	27	2	2	3	3	4	2	4	9	5	9	9	9	9	9	0	40	31	3	6	89	6	0	17	0	3	0	12
28	28	2	1	3	5	6	4	5	5	5	6	6	6	6	6	0	35	44	2	-9	85	-9	-9	-9	0	8	1	24
29	29	2	1	3	3	3	3	5	9	9	6	6	6	6	7	0	45	55	5	7	104	2	0	36	0	4	0	16
30	30	2	0	2	5	5	5	3	5	3	5	5	5	5	5	0	10	30	8	3	-9	11	-9	-9	0	3	0	24
31	31	1	0	3	5	5	2	4	4	2	2	2	2	2	2	1	47	47	7	5	110	3	0	36	-9	5	0	24
32	32	1	1	3	3	5	4	6	5	5	5	5	5	5	5	0	23	23	7	8	89	11	0	5	0	2	0	24
33	33	1	1	3	5	5	5	5	6	6	6	6	6	6	5	0	18	18	5	7	98	3	0	27	0	4	0	24
34	34	1	2	2	2	3	2	2	2	2	2	2	2	2	2	0	47	47	8	8	101	7	0	25	0	2	0	24

VARIABLES (continued)

1	2	3	4	5	6	7	8	9	10	11	12	13	14	15	16	17	18	19	20	21	22	23	24	25	26	27	28
35	1	2	2	2	2	6	6	6	7	6	6	6	8	8	1	35	12	7	3	95	12	1	10	0	8	0	24
36	1	2	3	3	3	5	6	5	5	6	8	8	8	8	1	55	17	7	2	100	3	0	45	0	3	0	24
37	2	2	3	3	3	3	5	2	2	2	2	2	9	2	0	35	41	5	5	110	2	0	10	0	3	0	24
38	1	2	3	3	7	6	-9	-9	-9	-9	-9	-9	-9	-9	1	20	-9	5	-9	-9	-9	-9	-9	-9	4	1	8
39	1	2	4	4	5	5	6	6	6	6	6	8	9	8	1	35	48	7	3	105	7	0	30	0	7	0	24
40	1	2	2	2	2	2	2	2	2	2	5	7	8	8	1	19	45	2	7	98	4	1	15	0	2	0	24
41	1	2	2	3	3	5	6	5	5	5	5	5	5	5	0	27	22	5	5	125	13	-9	44	0	6	0	24
42	1	2	2	2	2	3	2	1	1	1	1	-9	-9	-9	0	25	24	5	5	-9	-9	1	-9	-9	4	0	18
43	1	2	2	3	5	2	3	3	4	3	4	3	4	3	0	35	30	5	3	108	3	0	50	1	2	0	24
44	1	2	2	2	2	2	2	5	6	7	7	6	7	5	1	44	60	5	3	92	0	0	12	0	4	0	24
45	1	2	2	2	3	5	5	6	6	7	7	8	8	9	1	55	12	4	1	100	3	0	37	0	9	1	24
46	2	2	2	6	2	3	2	2	2	3	3	4	4	4	0	44	56	7	-9	135	3	0	20	0	2	0	24
47	2	2	3	4	2	2	7	-9	-9	-9	-9	-9	-9	-9	1	19	-9	8	6	120	10	0	50	1	7	1	10
48	2	2	2	3	4	5	5	5	5	5	5	5	5	5	1	30	35	6	6	97	1	0	25	0	3	0	24
49	2	2	2	1	1	1	5	4	6	6	6	6	6	7	0	55	20	9	3	100	6	0	44	0	7	0	24
50	2	2	3	3	3	2	5	2	4	4	5	5	2	5	0	44	40	7	6	123	7	0	30	0	2	0	24
51	2	2	3	3	3	3	1	2	2	2	1	2	2	1	0	45	52	7	7	98	4	0	27	0	3	0	24
52	2	2	4	4	2	2	3	6	3	3	3	1	1	1	0	30	27	5	5	114	10	0	20	0	3	0	24
53	2	2	2	5	3	3	3	3	3	3	3	2	2	2	0	27	23	4	3	100	2	-9	18	0	4	1	24
54	2	2	5	2	4	3	3	7	7	2	2	2	2	2	1	15	30	3	3	-9	-9	0	-9	-9	4	0	24
55	2	2	2	5	5	6	6	2	2	2	2	1	1	1	0	20	25	4	8	127	4	0	22	-9	8	1	24
56	2	2	3	2	2	2	2	1	1	1	1	1	1	1	1	22	-9	4	-9	-9	-9	-9	-9	-9	7	0	10
57	2	2	2	3	5	5	5	7	7	7	7	7	7	7	0	45	43	5	5	110	3	0	7	0	2	1	24
58	2	2	5	5	5	7	7	7	7	7	7	7	7	-9	1	10	7	2	1	105	12	1	2	0	6	0	24
59	2	2	4	4	2	2	4	5	6	6	8	6	5	-9	1	20	35	7	7	112	1	0	23	0	5	0	20
60	2	2	3	2	2	2	2	6	6	6	6	6	6	1	1	30	33	4	3	90	3	0	39	0	8	1	24

1 = Patient ID
2 = Child development (1 = no, 2 = yes)
3 = Family therapy (1 = no, 2 = yes)
4 - 15 = Dysphoria scores
16 = Mother's caseness

17-18 = Duration of mother–child interaction
19-20 = Ratings of emotional closeness
21 = Child IQ
22 = Child's depression score
23 = Child's caseness of depression

24 = Child's agression score
25 = Child's caseness for agression
26 = Marital conflict
27 = Husband's psychiatric history
28 = Weeks in study

Index